Fun Folds

Language Learning through Paper Folding

by Laura Grey and Rachel Katz

Illustrations by David Dame

Communication Skill Builders ®

3830 E. Bellevue/P.O. Box 42050
Tucson, Arizona 85733
(602) 323-7500

Duplicating

You may prefer to copy the designated reproducible materials by using stencils or spirit masters. It is not necessary to tear pages out of this book. Make a single photocopy of the desired page. Use that photocopy to make a stencil or spirit master on a thermal copier.

Communication Skill Builders, Inc.
3830 E. Bellevue/P.O. Box 42050
Tucson, Arizona 85733
(602) 323-7500

ISBN 0-88450-888-9   Catalog No. 7200

10 9 8 7 6 5 4
Printed in the United States of America

About the Authors

Laura Grey is a speech-language pathologist in the Merrick (New York) Union Free School District. Her responsibility encompasses diagnosis and remediation of students with speech and language deficits. She has helped to expand the district's Language Arts Curriculum and serves as a consultant to other districts in fields of diagnosis and remediation of language instruction. Mrs. Grey holds a B.A. degree from Brooklyn College, M.S. degree from Purdue University, and has continued her graduate studies at Adelphi University. She is certified as a teacher of Speech and Hearing Handicapped; teacher of Nursery, Kindergarten, and Grades 1-6; and is licensed as a Speech Pathologist in New York State. Mrs. Grey holds the American Speech-Language-Hearing Association's Certificate of Clinical Competence.

Rachel Katz is an Assistant Curator of the Origami Center of America. She has taught for the New York City Board of Education, and has conducted origami classes at libraries, schools, and museums throughout the New York metropolitan area; and for the Nassau and Suffolk County Boards of Cooperative Educational Services; and Hofstra University, Southampton College, and Dowling College. She is a consultant for New York State Arts in Education, and is a contributing artist to the American Museum of Natural History and to the Japan Air Lines Annual Exhibit, New York City. She holds a New York State teaching license in "common branches" and has a B.A. degree from Hunter College.

Contents

Preface

Several years ago, I observed a fascinating lesson in the art of paper folding demonstrated by Rachel Katz, an assistant curator of the Origami Center of America in New York City. Three classes of primary students sat enthralled as Mrs. Katz told a story which she illustrated with paper models created from a single sheet of newspaper. After the lesson, the special education students with whom I was working insisted on recreating the art forms we had observed. Thus, we began a step-by-step process of producing a paper project, listing each step on a spirit master so the students could share the activity with their families. The outstanding remedial and educational features of this activity, not to mention the enjoyment and interest factor, became apparent to me as I worked with these now highly motivated students. Soon after, I scheduled a meeting with Rachel Katz so that I might learn to make additional paper models as a stimulating educational learning experience for my students. It occurred to me that the paper folds would be a good device for teaching language. The *Fun Folds* program is an outgrowth of our collaboration in the paper-folding art form.

Laura Grey

Introduction

Fun Folds is a creative format for teaching language. Through use of this paper-folding art form, language teaching gains a new dimension. Learning becomes active, rather than passive. This multisensory, multidimensional program helps children develop temporal-spatial concepts and expand oral expression, auditory and visual memory and sequencing skills, visual-motor proficiency, and receptive and expressive language skills as they participate in an enjoyable, stimulating, and interesting paper-folding activity.

Presenting concepts both visually and auditorily provides a sound clinical teaching technique. Development of specific auditory and visual attention and memory skills are basic to academic learning. Auditory and visual attentive skills are fostered by the need to attend to the teacher's step-by-step presentation leading to completing an exciting project. Those skills are reinforced when the students become aware of the positive results of attentive behavior.

Auditory memory skills are developed when the students orally review the sequence of steps necessary to complete a *Fun Folds* project. Visual memory skills develop as the students use similar folding patterns to develop various projects. Also, the students can be taught to close their eyes as the teacher reviews each step necessary for completing the fold. This revisualization helps in building visual memory and sequencing skills.

Development of receptive and expressive skills occurs as the students develop an understanding of the basic concepts necessary to complete a *Fun Folds* project. Through hearing the directions and completing the fold, words take on a new dimension. This motor activity accompanied by verbalization provides significant language comprehension and expression.

The *Fun Folds* program allows the students to become active participants in the learning process. It provides them with the opportunity to plan, comprehend, and ultimately produce a creative project. This helps them to build confidence and a desire to continue the learning process. Paper folding appeals to the play instinct as a method of stimulating children to learn.

The clearly written descriptive text accompanying each diagram allows not only for simple, teacher-directed lessons, but also for a successful self-directed activity for intermediate-level students. Often, students from speech/language classes return to the classroom with creative ideas for preparing bulletin boards. They present demonstration lessons and share information on paper-folding projects with their classmates. Classroom teachers find these activities valuable, and they ask for additional projects to prepare with their classes.

Thus, the enthusiasm and interest we have encountered from classroom teachers, special educators, resource room teachers, and speech/language pathologists led to the creation of the language-oriented curriculum units accompanied by *Fun Folds*. We believe its value as a unique, creative, exciting, and stimulating educational tool will enhance your programs and foster student growth.

The Lesson Plan Guide

Objectives

To develop auditory and visual attention skills

To develop temporal-spatial concepts

To develop visual-motor skills

To develop auditory and visual sequencing skills

To teach the concepts and vocabulary that are listed for each *Fun Folds* model

Materials

A list of appropriate, readily available materials necessary to complete the fold is listed for each *Fun Folds* model.

Procedure

The models in each unit are arranged in order of difficulty. Pictures and text provide step-by-step instruction.

Give verbal directions as you demonstrate each step.

Follow-up suggestions

See the Language, Social Studies, Science, and Speech Activities relating to each unit.

Have the students close their eyes and revisualize each step of the *Fun Folds* procedure as you recount the steps.

Make an experience chart emphasizing the sequential aspects of the lesson.

Use *Fun Folds* on the bulletin board or on greeting cards.

Have the students teach the *Fun Folds* to others. This activity fosters socialization while emphasizing speech and language development.

Additional suggestions

Additional curriculum-oriented follow-up activities are given for individual *Fun Folds*.

Meeting Lesson Plan Objectives

The language-oriented curriculum was developed to provide the classroom teacher or specialist with a general framework from which to "slot" activities. Many of the activities were chosen to augment and enhance *Fun Folds* projects and, at the same time, provide specific activities in the development of the primary students' auditory, verbal, visual, and motor growth. The professional is encouraged to expand or modify these activities according to the students' capabilities, curriculum requirements, and grade level placement.

The following skill development format is provided to augment both the *Fun Folds* and language-oriented curriculum lessons provided in each unit.

Receptive and expressive vocabulary. Vocabulary growth is fostered when children are provided with experiences for which they develop inner labels. Expressive vocabulary growth occurs when children utilize these inner labels to manipulate their environment and express their needs.

Auditory attention. By providing stimulating and interesting lessons, we will develop the student's ability to attend to material presented orally.

Auditory closure. The student will develop the ability to complete an incomplete thought, sentence, or story.

Auditory memory. The student will develop the ability to retain and recall words and events.

Auditory sequencing. Reviewing the steps necessary to complete a *Fun Folds* model develops the student's ability to retain and recall information in appropriate order.

Oral language structure. Various language exercises are suggested for each unit and provide the student with practice in speaking in grammatically correct sentences.

Auditory comprehension. Through active participation in creating a *Fun Folds* model, the student develops auditory comprehension skills.

Visual attention. The student must attend as the teacher demonstrates each step in preparing the *Fun Folds*.

Visual memory. The student will develop the ability to retain and recall the steps in preparing the *Fun Folds*.

Visual sequencing. Reviewing the steps necessary to complete a fold develops the student's ability to retain and recall information in appropriate order.

Visual-motor integration. Completion of a fold requires the relating of a motor act to a visually presented clue.

Temporal-spatial concepts. The ability to understand the position of the self, and objects with relation to each other, is fostered when completing a *Fun Folds* model.

Social studies and science activities also are provided with a view toward assisting the teacher or specialist with an effective and comprehensive learning program.

Activities also are provided for speech remediation. These activities are flexible and allow for creative interpretation, expansion, and adaptation by the speech-language pathologist.

Folding Concepts

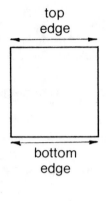

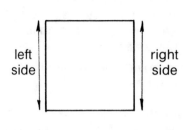

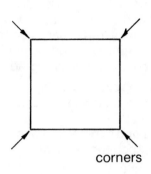
corners

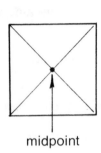
midpoint

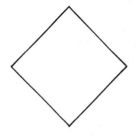
Square placed down so it
looks like a diamond.

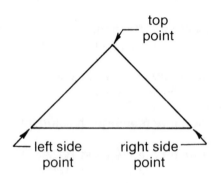

Vocabulary

Spatial Concepts

upper	top	
lower	bottom	
front	side	
back	edge	
inside	corner	
outside	underneath	
outer	left	
inner	right	
behind	forward	
beside	backward	
between	toward	
center	away from	
midpoint	up	
point	down	
upside down	upward	
opposite	downward	

Action Concepts (verbs)

draw
lift
pull
push
pinch
tuck
press
press flat
crease
open
fold
unfold
repeat
turn
turn over

Quantitative Concepts

long
short
wide
narrow

Geometric Concepts

shape
square
rectangle
diamond
triangle

Miscellaneous

meet
flap
layer
as shown

Symbols

white side of the paper

colored side of the paper

— — — — — valley fold

valley fold

—·—·—·— mountain fold

mountain fold

turn over

fold and unfold

fold in this direction   —   see "valley fold" above

fold backward   —   see "mountain fold" above

————— crease made previously

✂ cut

Helpful Hints

1. Select an appropriate model to teach. *Fun Folds* have been arranged within curriculum units according to difficulty. The easier ones are presented first.

2. Select paper that will enhance the model. See "Developing Creativity/ Selection of Materials."

3. You will find it easier to follow the diagrams if you use paper that is colored on one side only. The shading in the diagrams corresponds to the colored side.

4. Try the model before you teach it. Make a sample with the paper you intend to have the students use, so you can anticipate any problems that might arise.

5. Encourage students to keep their papers flat on the table. Whenever paper is lifted, there is a likelihood for error if it is not placed down exactly as it was before.

6. Teach right and left. Have the students raise their right hands and locate the right side of their papers. Repeat with the left hand.

7. Elaborate on the verbal instructions. Explain each step in many ways. For example, say "Fold the corner up, away from you, to the top" or "Put the crease straight up and down, vertically, like the number one."

8. Always look ahead to the next step to see the fold completed.

9. Make a "permanent press." When creasing the paper, press gently, check the fold, and then "permanent press" with thumbnail to sharpen the crease.

10. Encourage neatness. Careful folding—especially at the beginning of a model—is important.

See also: "Symbols," and "Folding Concepts," and "Working with Younger Children."

Working with Younger Children (Grades K-2)

1. It is preferable to have all the children seated facing in one direction.

2. Select appropriate models to teach. Folds that begin with a triangle are good ones to start with. Refer to the triangle as having "a head and two arms." By visualizing this, the children should be able to orient their triangles correctly.

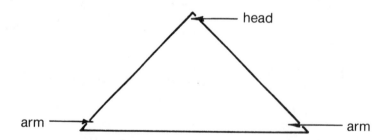

3. Demonstrate the steps. Always fold in the same direction as the students. When facing them, mirror their movements.

4. Avoid terms "right" and "left." Since laterality is not generally internalized in this age group, substitute the words "fold one side, fold the other side" for "fold the left side, fold the right side."

See also: "Symbols," "Folding Concepts," and "Helpful Hints."

Developing Creativity

Paper folding can be a creative art form. Selecting or coloring of the paper, creating new folds, and putting the completed models to use are all part of the creative process.

Paper is an ideal medium to work with because it comes in a wide variety of colors and textures. Since it is plentiful and inexpensive, paper usually can be used freely without concern for waste.

Selecting Suitable Materials

Third class mail. Don't overlook this free source of materials! Many advertising brochures make wonderful models.

Magazine pages. Magazines are filled with colorful pictures and advertisements which, when cut into squares and folded, make colorful flowers and birds.

Stationery. Writing paper with interesting textures and designs is available in individual sheets or pads. Usually it is rectangular, requiring just one cut to make it square.

Typing paper. Typing paper is ideal because it is easily available, is thin, can be painted or colored, and creases well.

Used duplicating paper. Don't throw it away! This is a wonderful free source of useful teaching material. It's printed on one side, allowing you to see if the students have turned the paper over correctly when required to do so.

Newspaper or blank newsprint. This material is ideal because it is so inexpensive and comes in large sizes. It is especially good for hats, but not suitable where stiff paper is required.

Construction paper. This paper is colorful, readily available, and helpful when tiny fingers need something solid to grasp. Since it is rather thick, the finished model may need to be stapled or taped to hold it flat.

Paper-backed foil (gift wrap). Beautiful models can be made with paper-backed foil, but it is rather expensive and difficult to cut if purchased on a roll.

Gift wrap paper. Gift wrap makes beautiful models. It is much easier to use if purchased in flat sheets.

Origami paper. This paper is sold in packages of precut squares, colored on one side and white on the other. It can be purchased in art supply stores or Oriental import shops, but it is relatively expensive compared to other paper.

Various art papers. These papers are usually ideal to work with, especially if thin and crisp.

Store bags. Grocery bags are generally too thick to fold, but other store bags often are surprisingly attractive and thin enough for folding.

Notebook paper. Notebook paper is inexpensive and readily available, making it ideal for practice.

Poster paper. This thinner version of construction paper works well. Do not use old paper, however, because it may crack when folded.

Tracing paper. This thin, crisp paper is ideal for making birds.

Shelf paper. Shelf paper is available in a variety of colors and designs. Experiment to find papers that are not too heavily coated to fold well.

Crepe paper. Crepe paper generally will not hold a crease, but it is useful for making hats. Staples will be needed to hold the finished hat together.

Tissue paper. This paper is suitable for models where you wish to stretch the paper (for example, the butterfly). Be careful, though—it is very thin and tears easily!

This list is by no means complete. Experiment with any paper at hand. You might try butcher paper, greeting cards, paper napkins, or computer paper. There are no rules in paper selection. Let your artistic sense be your guide.

Creating Your Own Fun Folds

Children constantly surprise us with their creativity. They are less inhibited than adults. They look at a triangle and see a mountain, or they bend the sides around and call it a hat. Their imaginations fill in all the details. It's wonderful to see them take such pleasure in their own creations. In fact, several models in this book were inspired by young folders.

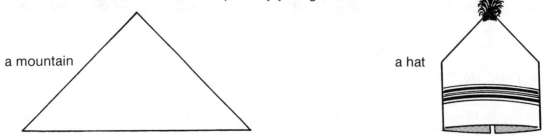

a mountain   a hat

Fun Folds projects are designed to produce a particular result; but once a model has been learned, see what else it can become! The whale turned sideways looks like the head of a bird. The ice-cream cone turned upside down becomes a face with a hat; turn it over, and it's a kite.

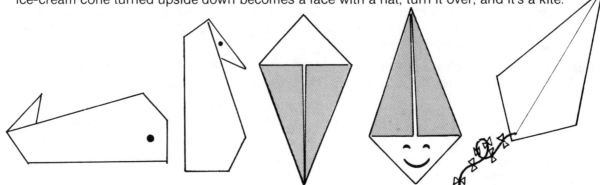

Paper folding need not be complex to be charming and satisfying. Forget your inhibitions, and you too can create your own *Fun Folds!*

Using Fun Folds in Different Ways

Greeting cards. The heart will enhance a Mother's Day or Valentine's Day card, and a whale makes a card for "A whale of a Dad." Boats, doves, and swans make lovely additions to cards.

Invitations. Many models are suitable for this purpose. For example:

Won't you come to my party?
"Whale" have lots of fun.
Name: _____
Date: _____
Time: _____
Address: _____

Party baskets. The May basket or Easter basket is suitable for filling with party goodies.

Party games. The jumping frog can be used competitively. Have the contestants "jump" their frogs into a box.

Have sailboat races. Blow sailboats gently across a smooth surface.

Airplane-flying contests are always fun. Fly planes for distance, and measure time in flight with a stopwatch.

Party favors and centerpieces. Large models—for example, swans—can be used as centerpieces, while miniatures of the same model make delightful party favors.

Christmas tree decorations. Paper-folded creations can be used to adorn Christmas trees. In 1981, the tree in the Blue Room of the White House was covered with paper-folded models. Candy canes, whales, and swans are particularly suitable.

Place cards. Boats, horses, boots, and many other *Fun Folds* models make novel place cards.

Mobiles. Imagine a mobile of colorful butterflies or birds! Build your mobile from the bottom up. Straws or wires work well as a support for the folded models.

Bulletin boards. Any season can be highlighted with a *Fun Folds* bulletin board. Use colorful tulips to usher in spring, or sailboats to "sail into summer."

Puppets. Puppets can be made from many animal models. Use them for role playing, creative drama, or just for fun.

Cross-Reference Chart

Fun Folds	Animals	Seasons	Holidays	Transportation	Water Life	Language	Social Studies	Science	Reading	Speech	Mathematics
Airplane				X		X		X	X	X	X
Alligator	X				X	X			X	X	X
Basic Bird	X					X			X	X	X
Basic Sailboat				X	X	X			X	X	X
Basic Dog	X					X			X	X	X
Boot		X	X	X		X			X	X	X
Butterfly	X	X				X			X	X	X
"Candle-Folded" Napkin			X			X		X	X	X	X
Candy Cane			X			X			X	X	X
Canoe				X	X	X	X		X	X	X
Cat	X					X			X	X	X
Colonial Bonnet			X			X	X		X	X	X
Crab	X				X	X			X	X	X
Dove	X					X			X	X	X
Fan		X				X			X	X	X
Fish	X				X	X			X	X	X
Flag			X			X	X		X	X	X
Flower		X	X			X		X	X	X	X
Frog	X				X	X		X	X	X	X
Goldfish	X				X	X			X	X	X
Halloween Masks			X			X			X	X	X
Heart			X			X			X	X	X
Helicopter				X		X	X	X	X	X	X
Horse	X			X		X	X		X	X	X
Kite		X				X		X	X	X	X
May Basket		X				X			X	X	X
New Year's Hat			X			X			X	X	X
Notebook		X				X			X	X	X
Pecking Bird	X					X		X	X	X	X
Pelican	X				X	X			X	X	X
Penguin	X				X	X	X	X	X	X	X
Picture Frame			X			X			X	X	X
Pig	X					X		X	X	X	X
Rabbit	X		X			X		X	X	X	X
Rocket Ship				X		X		X	X	X	X

Fun Folds	Animals	Seasons	Holidays	Transportation	Water Life	Language	Social Studies	Science	Reading	Speech	Mathematics
Rowboat				X	X	X	X		X	X	X
Sailboat (Double Sail)			X	X	X	X	X	X	X	X	X
Sailboat (Single Sail)		X		X	X	X			X	X	X
Sailor with Hat			X	X	X	X	X		X	X	X
Sled		X		X		X	X	X	X	X	X
Snowflake		X				X	X	X	X	X	X
Swan	X				X	X			X	X	X
Talking Dog	X					X			X	X	X
Tulip		X	X			X		X	X	X	X
Viking Hat					X	X	X		X	X	X
Wagon				X		X	X		X	X	X
Whale	X				X	X		X	X	X	X
Wolf	X					X			X	X	X

Animals

The Lesson Plan Guide

Objectives

To develop auditory and visual attention skills

To develop temporal-spatial concepts

To develop visual-motor skills

To develop auditory and visual sequencing skills

To teach the concepts and vocabulary that are listed for each model in addition to those listed on page 4

Procedure

Give verbal directions as you demonstrate each step.

Follow-up suggestions

See the Language, Social Studies, Science, and Speech Activities related to the Animals unit (pp. 16-21).

Have the students close their eyes and revisualize each step of the *Fun Folds* as you recount the steps.

Make an experience chart emphasizing the sequential aspects of the lesson.

Have the students teach the *Fun Folds* to others. This activity fosters socialization while emphasizing speech and language development.

Use the *Fun Folds* on the bulletin board or on greeting cards.

Additional suggestions

Additional curriculum-oriented follow-up activities are given for individual *Fun Folds*.

Language Activities

These activities develop vocabulary, thinking skills, comprehension, and expression of language. Encourage students to reply in a complete sentence. It may be necessary to repeat the students' answers in expanded sentence form until they begin to respond appropriately.

1. Mount pictures of animals on squares of sandpaper which will adhere to a flannel board. Label the animals and group them into appropriate categories. Label and discuss the various environments in which they are found.

   Farm animals: horse, pig, chicken, sheep, . . .

   Wild animals: lion, tiger, elephant, giraffe, . . .

   Baby animals: piglet, calf, lamb, chick, cub, . . .

   Forest animals: squirrel, deer, owl, bear, . . .

   Desert animals: lizard, snake, camel, . . .

   Pets: dog, cat, bird, hamster, . . .

   Insects: butterfly, grasshopper, bee, . . .

   Animal homes: jungle, forest, farm, zoo, . . .

   Animal houses: corral, pen, coop, hutch, cave, den, . . .

2. Use the following vocabulary to describe animals. Encourage the students to add words to the list and use them in sentences. The students then can draw pictures to illustrate the sentences.

   Adjectives: ugly, angry, fierce, soft, purring, fuzzy, shaggy, graceful, beautiful, funny, fat, . . .

   Irregular past tense verbs:

run - ran	ride - rode	fly - flew
bite - bit	catch - caught	creep - crept
grow - grew	feed - fed	spring - sprang - sprung

   Irregular plural nouns:

wolf - wolves	calf - calves	hoof - hooves
goose - geese	sheep - sheep	deer - deer
butterfly - butterflies		

3. Antonyms. Write antonym word pairs on *Fun Folds* dog, rabbit, fox, and cat ears.

wild - tame	land - sea	carnivorous - herbivorous
young - old	long - short	dangerous - safe
hunter - prey	capture - free	gentle - rough

4. Synonyms.

violent - rough	gentle - kind	dangerous - harmful
capture - seize	free - loose	hunt - chase

5. Homographs. The students can illustrate and write sentences that show the multiple meanings of words (for example, A bat lives in a cave; Hit the ball with the bat).

fly	bark	calf
trunk	pet	steer
seal	perch	horn

6. Homonyms. Have the students draw pictures or write sentences that show meanings of homonyms.

mane - main - Maine	horse - hoarse	fowl - foul
deer - dear	herd - heard	tail - tale
bee - be	bear - bare	hare - hair
prey - pray	paws - pause	meat - meet

7. Similarities and differences. Have the students explain how these animals are the same and how they are different:

cow - pig	chicken - duck	dog - bird
horse - zebra	sheep - turkey	lion - cat
fish - turtle	squirrel - bear	rooster - hen

8. Categories. This activity develops auditory memory, comprehension, and oral language skills. Have the students repeat each group of words after you. Ask them which word does not belong. Have them explain their choices. (Note: For young students, use picture cards to augment oral presentation.)

lion - tiger - elephant - lamb
piglet - puppy - horse - kitten
meat - carrot - lamb - pork
chick - rooster - dog - hen
squirrel - bear - elephant - deer
feathers - fur - scales - giraffe

9. Analogies. This activity develops auditory attention skills, auditory association, auditory closure, and oral expression. It also can be presented as a written exercise to develop visual closure skills. Read the following analogies aloud, emphasizing the key word in each analogy. This will help the students to focus more clearly on the correct solution.

Animal-to-part relationships:

Rhinoceros is to **horn** as elephant is to _____. (tusk)

Dog is to **paw** as horse is to _____. (hoof)

Person is to **mouth** as parrot is to _____. (beak)

Fish is to **fin** as bird is to _____. (wing)

Ram is to **horn** as deer is to _____. (antlers)

Fish is to **scales** as dog is to _____. (fur)

Leopard is to **spots** as zebra is to _____. (stripes)

Mothers and their babies:

Cow is to **calf** as horse is to _____. (foal)

Dog is to **puppy** as cat is to _____. (kitten)

Pig is to **piglet** as sheep is to _____. (lamb)

Duck is to **duckling** as goose is to _____. (gosling)

Bear is to **cub** as deer is to _____. (fawn)

Hen is to **chick** as goat is to _____. (kid)

Animal sounds:

Donkey is to **hee-haw** as pig is to _____. (oink)

Dog is to **bark** as cat is to _____. (meow)

Cow is to **moo** as lamb is to _____. (baa)

Chicken is to **cluck** as frog is to _____. (croak)

Duck is to **quack** as bird is to _____. (chirp)

Animal homes:

Bear is to **cave** as owl is to _____ . (tree)

Pig is to **pen** as horse is to _____ . (corral)

Rabbit is to **hutch** as chicken is to _____ . (coop)

Duck is to **pond** as whale is to _____ . (ocean)

Lion is to **jungle** as cow is to _____ . (farm)

Squirrel is to **forest** as rattlesnake is to _____ . (desert)

10. "Clue" Game. This activity develops auditory attention, auditory memory, auditory comprehension, and oral language skills. You may use picture cards of animals to aid the student in thinking of appropriate clues. Some examples are:

    I have a long trunk. I am big and gray. I like peanuts. What am I?

    I have a mane and hooves. I live on the farm. People like to ride me. What am I?

    I am a pet. I am furry. I bark. What am I?

    I use my tail as an extra hand. I live in trees. I eat bananas. What am I?

    I have a long neck. I eat leaves from the tops of trees. I have blotches and spots on my coat. What am I?

11. Idioms. This activity develops comprehension of language. Have the students illustrate the literal and figurative meanings of the following idioms. These drawings can make a creative bulletin board.

    packed in like sardines

    eat like a bird

    quit horsing around

    a frog in my throat

    let the cat out of the bag

    wild goose chase

    let sleeping dogs lie

    a fish out of water

    it's raining cats and dogs

12. Comparatives. Make *Fun Folds* pig, cat, and rabbit. Teach the concept of *long, longer, longest.* (Refer to animals' ears.)

13. Crossword puzzle and word scramble. This activity develops visual sequencing, visual memory, and visual-motor skills. Reproduce and distribute the worksheet on the following page.

    Answer key: DOWN—pig, hen, goat, bird, calf, owl, fox

    ACROSS—penguin, dog, cat, wolf, colt

"Animals" Worksheet

Name _____ Date _____

Directions: Unscramble the "Animals" words.
Then, using the letter clues, fill in the Dog Crossword Puzzle.

DOWN	**ACROSS**
gip	nepuign
ehn	gdo
ogta	tca
drib	folw
aflc	tolc
olw	
ofx	

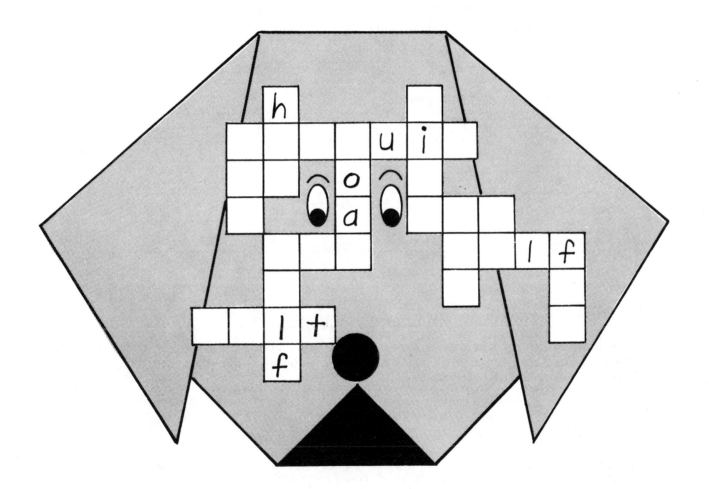

Social Studies Activities

1. Prepare dioramas showing animals in their natural environments.

2. Make a circus train, using shoe boxes.

3. Visit the zoo and discuss animals in their natural habitats.

4. Visit a local pet shop and discuss the tame animals you observe.

5. Discuss and locate geographical origins of animals.

6. Prepare a map and mount pictures of native animals.

Science Activities

1. Discuss animals and the food they provide.

   Chickens lay eggs.

   Turkeys and chickens are fowl that we eat.

   Cows give us milk, butter, cheese, and cream.

   We get bacon, pork, and ham from pigs.

   We get meat from steers.

2. Classify animals by their eating habits.

Herbivores (plant eaters)	Carnivores (meat eaters)
giraffe	lion
rabbit	tiger
cow	dog
goat	cat
pig	wolf
horse	bear

Speech Activities

The following are excellent as carryover activities for articulation therapy, choral speaking, voice therapy, and fluency practice. They also develop auditory sequencing, auditory memory, comprehension, and oral expression skills.

1. Have students teach the animal *Fun Folds* to others. This activity provides an opportunity for students to practice tension-free vocal quality and improve pitch, volume, and rate. Children who stutter can build confidence as they practice fluent speech.

2. Have the children mount *Fun Folds* on tongue depressors, to make puppets. Then they can dramatize stories (*The Three Little Pigs, Three Little Kittens,* and others).

3. Have the students make appropriate *Fun Folds* animals and sing *Old MacDonald Had a Farm* and *The Old Woman Who Swallowed a Fly,* emphasizing their sequential aspects.

4. If possible, video-tape the students' performance on the above activities. This is an effective teaching and therapy technique.

5. Play "Animal Fishing Game." Make two sets of cards by mounting duplicate sets of animal pictures (or *Peel & Put*® stickers) on squares of construction paper. Distribute one set of cards among the players. On the other set, attach a paper clip to each card and place the cards face down on the table. Attach a magnet to a string suspended from a stick, and give it to the first player to "go fishing." The student says, " I went to the zoo to see the _____ ." When a matching animal is "caught," the student may ask another student, "May I have your _____ ?" The student then takes another turn.

6. Play "Animal Homes." Mount pictures of an aquarium, zoo, farm, and circus on construction paper. Then mount pictures of animals containing target sounds (lion, seal, rhinoceros, etc.) on small squares of paper. Prop up the animal environment pictures. Select an animal picture containing the target sound, and hide it behind one of the environment pictures. Have the students guess the animal's location ("Is the *seal* in the *circus*?"). The student who guesses correctly takes the next turn.

Basic Dog

This fold is ideal for younger children. There are few steps and no complicated folds. It can be taught using the terms "one side" and "the other side" instead of "right side" and "left side."

Concepts and vocabulary (*See also* page 4)

head

arm

ear

dog

mouth

little

form

face

floppy

Materials

A triangle of thin paper, cut from a square on the diagonal

A pencil, marking pen, or crayon

An additional suggestion

Discuss different breeds of dogs (collie, German shepherd, boxer, others).

How to fold the Basic Dog

1. Begin with a triangle of paper.

   Your triangle has a head and two arms.

2. Put the triangle on the table so the head is pointing down.

3. Fold one arm down to form an ear, as shown.

4. Do the same thing to form the other ear, as shown.

5. Fold the bottom point up a little bit to make a mouth.

6. Draw the dog's face.

   You have made a dog with floppy ears!

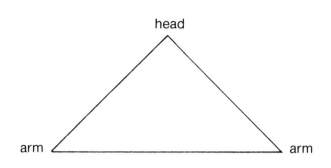

1 Begin with a triangle of paper.
Your triangle has a head and two arms.

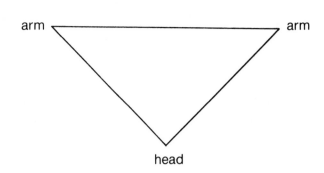

2 Put the triangle on the table so the head is pointing down.

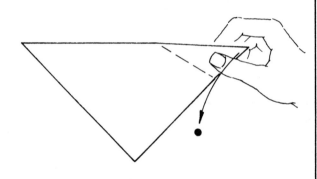

3 Fold one arm down to form an ear, as shown.

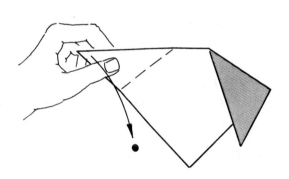

4 Do the same thing to form the other ear, as shown.

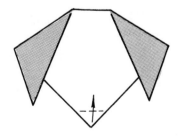

5 Fold the bottom point up a little bit to make a mouth.

6 Draw the dog's face.
You have made a dog with floppy ears!

Basic Bird
(Also: Butterfly)

This fold is ideal for very young children. There are few steps and no complicated folds. It can be taught using the terms "one side" and "the other side" instead of "right side" and "left side."

Concepts and vocabulary (*See also* page 4)

wings

head

arm

only

move

bird

butterfly

Materials

A triangle of very thin paper, cut from a square on the diagonal

An additional suggestion

Discuss other winged creatures.

How to fold the Basic Bird

1. Place a triangle of paper on the table so the head is pointing to one side.
   Fold the bottom arm up to meet the top arm.

2. Make sure that the folded edge is at the bottom.
   Now fold up the folded edge a little bit.

3. It looks like a boat.
   Now unfold the crease you just made.

4. Using only the top layer, fold down the point, making use of the crease on your paper.

5. It looks like this.
   Turn it over and fold down the other wing the same way.

6. Hold the bird underneath, and move your arm up and down to make the wings move.

To make a butterfly

Follow the same procedure, using a much smaller triangle.
Color the butterfly's wings, or use a brightly colored paper.

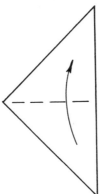

1 Place a triangle of paper on the table so the head is pointing to one side.

Fold the bottom arm up to meet the top arm.

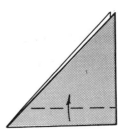

2 Make sure that the folded edge is at the bottom.

Now fold up the folded edge a little bit.

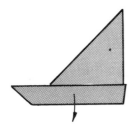

3 It looks like a boat.

Now unfold the crease you just made.

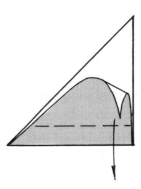

4 Using only the top layer, fold down the point, making use of the crease on your paper.

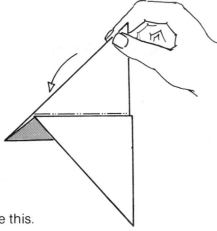

5 It looks like this.

Turn it over and fold down the other wing the same way.

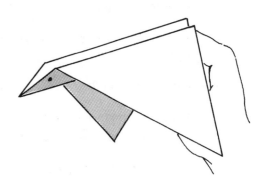

6 Hold the bird underneath, and move your arm up and down to make the wings move.

Dove

Hint

The cut in Step 4 is tricky. Make sure it is parallel to the breast of the bird. You may wish to mark the students' papers at the cut line and the dot.

Concepts and vocabulary (*See also* page 4)

index finger

beak

draw

near

cut

dot

eye

dotted line

tiny

only

Materials

A 6-inch square of thin paper

Scissors

A pencil

Additional suggestions

Fold several doves, and use them to make a mobile.

Doves can be used as Christmas tree ornaments.

Use the Dove as a stimulus for a unit on classifying birds.

How to fold the Dove

1. Put a square of paper on the table so it looks like a diamond.
   Fold the top point down to meet the bottom point.

2. Fold the top left point down in front. Crease. Unfold.
   Crease the same point behind. Unfold.

3. Put your index finger on the point and push the little triangle inside. Be sure the point (the beak) still shows.

4. Draw a line on the paper near the tail, as shown. Cut up to the dot.

5. Fold only the top layer up on the dotted line.
   Turn over and repeat behind.

6. Draw a tiny dot for an eye.

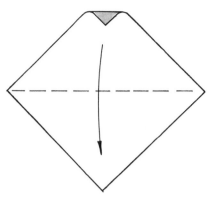

1 Put a square of paper on the table so it looks like a diamond.

Fold the top point down to meet the bottom point.

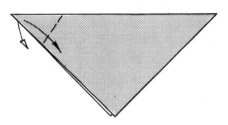

2 Fold the top left point down in front. Crease. Unfold.

Crease the same point behind. Unfold.

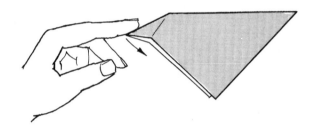

3 Put your index finger on the point and push the little triangle inside. Be sure the point (the beak) still shows.

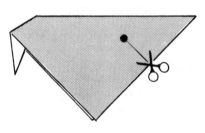

4 Draw a line on the paper near the tail, as shown. Cut up to the dot.

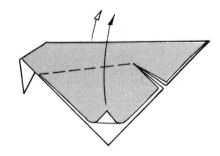

5 Fold only the top layer up on the dotted line. Turn over and repeat behind.

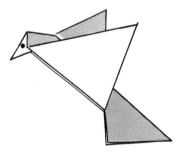

6 Draw a tiny dot for an eye.

Cat

This fold is ideal for younger children. There are few steps, and no complicated folds.

Hint

Teach the Basic Dog and the Tulip before you teach the Cat.

Concepts and vocabulary (*See also* page 4)

another

tulip

face

whiskers

cat

Materials

A triangle of paper, cut from a square on the diagonal

A pencil, marking pen, or crayon

An additional suggestion

Make other *Fun Folds* animals, and discuss animal sounds.

How to fold the Cat

1. Begin with a triangle of paper.
   Put the triangle on the table, as shown.

2. Fold one point up to the dot, as shown.

3. Repeat with the other point, as shown.

4. It looks like a tulip.

5. Fold the top point down to make another triangle.

6. It looks like this.

7. Turn over. Draw a face and whiskers.

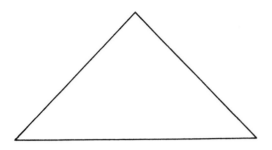

1 Begin with a triangle of paper. Put the triangle on the table, as shown.

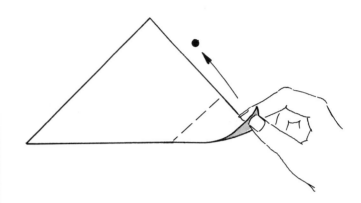

2 Fold one point up to the dot, as shown.

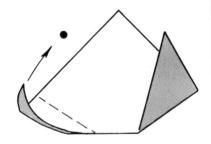

3 Repeat with the other point, as shown.

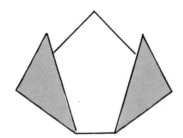

4 It looks like a tulip.

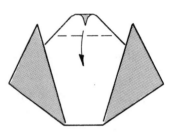

5 Fold the top point down to make another triangle.

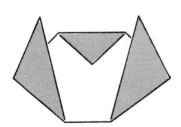

6 It looks like this.

7 Turn over. Draw a face and whiskers.

Talking Dog

With very young children, make the Basic Dog first.

If steps 1, 2, and 3 are done carefully, the finished model will open and close its mouth as you manipulate the paper. To do this, pinch the finished dog by putting your thumbs on the ears and your fingers on the back of the head. Move your hands together and apart.

Concepts and vocabulary (*See also* page 4)

  face

  ear

  mouth

  cover

  talking dog

Materials

  A 6-inch or larger square of thin paper

  A pencil, marking pens, or crayons

An additional suggestion

  Make the Pig and the Cat. Discuss similarities and differences in these *Fun Folds.*

How to fold the Talking Dog

1. Place a square of paper on the table so it looks like a diamond.
    Fold the left point over to meet the right point.

2. Unfold.

3. Fold the top point down to meet the bottom point.

4. Now there are two layers.
    Fold the top layer up a little bit, making a tiny triangle for a mouth.

5. Fold both the side corners down to the dots to form the ears, as shown. (The ears will cover part of the face.)

6. Draw a face.

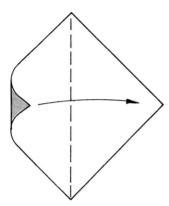

1 Place a square of paper on the table so it looks like a diamond.

Fold the left point over to meet the right point.

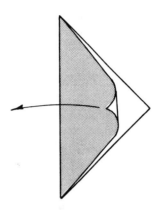

2 Unfold.

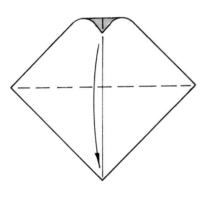

3 Fold the top point down to meet the bottom point.

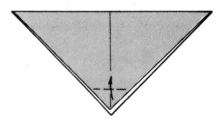

4 Now there are two layers.

Fold the top layer up a little bit, making a tiny triangle for a mouth.

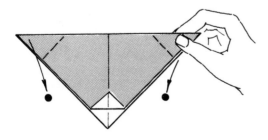

5 Fold both the side corners down to the dots to form the ears, as shown. (The ears will cover part of the face.)

6 Draw a face.

Wolf
(Also: Fox)

With very young children, the terms "one side" and "the other side" can be used instead of "right" and "left."

Concepts and vocabulary (*See also* page 4)

only

mouth

index finger

wolf

fox

Materials

A 6-inch or larger square of thin paper

A pencil, marking pen, or crayon

Additional suggestions

Make a mask, using a 12-inch square of paper. Cut out the eyes and use elastic to hold it in place on the child's face.

Fold the Basic Dog and the Fox, mount them on sticks, and present *The Fox and the Hound.*

Use the Wolf and three *Fun Folds* Pig puppets to dramatize *The Three Little Pigs.*

How to fold the Wolf

1. Put a square of paper on the table so it looks like a diamond.
   Fold the top point down to meet the bottom point.

2. Fold the left and right points down to meet the bottom point.

3. Put your index finger on the top point. Fold the lower right point up to the dot, as shown.

4. Repeat with the lower left point.

5. Turn over.

6. Look at the lower point. There are two layers. Fold only the top layer up on the dotted line (to make the mouth).
   Draw eyes.

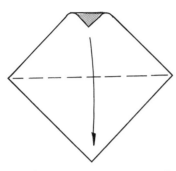

1 Put a square of paper on the table so it looks like a diamond.

Fold the top point down to meet the bottom point.

2 Fold the left and right points down to meet the bottom point.

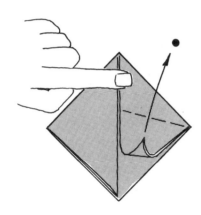

3 Put your index finger on the top point. Fold the lower right point up to the dot, as shown.

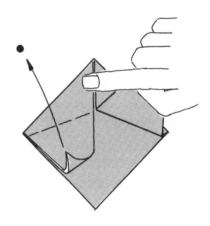

4 Repeat with the lower left point.

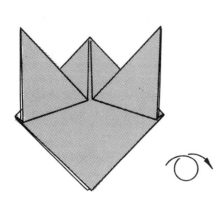

5 Turn over.

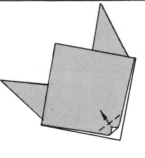

6 Look at the lower point. There are two layers. Fold only the top layer up on the dotted line (to make the mouth).

Draw eyes.

Pecking Bird

Hints

It may be helpful to refer to the center crease in Step 2 as a "stop line."

Since it is easier to fold paper up (away from you), you may wish to have the children fold the lower edges up, and then turn the paper around.

The finished bird will "peck" better if placed on a rough surface.

Concepts and vocabulary (*See also* page 4)

later

squeeze

balance

peck

gently

beak

bird

little

half

reach

tap

Materials

A 6-inch square of crisp paper

Additional suggestions

Stand the Pecking Bird up like a penguin and use it for a place card.

Make the Crab. The steps are almost the same as those used in this model.

How to fold the Pecking Bird

1. Put a square of paper on the table so it looks like a diamond.
   Fold the left point over to meet the right point. Crease. Unfold.

2. Fold the upper left and right sides down to meet the center crease.

3. Fold the top point down a little, as shown. (Later, this will become the beak.)

4. Fold the left side over to meet the right side. Now you have folded the model in half.

5. Reach inside and pull out the beak.

6. Squeeze or fold flat at the dot.

7. Balance the bird on its beak. Tap its tail gently to make it "peck."

1 Put a square of paper on the table so it looks like a diamond.
Fold the left point over to meet the right point. Crease. Unfold.

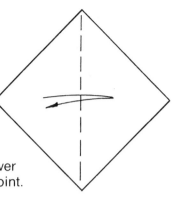

2 Fold the upper left and right sides down to meet the center crease.

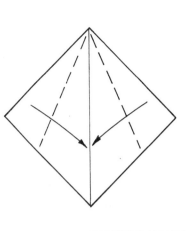

3 Fold the top point down a little, as shown. (Later, this will become the beak.)

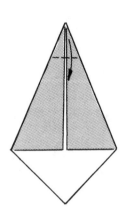

4 Fold the left side over to meet the right side. Now you have folded the model in half.

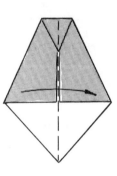

5 Reach inside and pull out the beak.

6 Squeeze or fold flat at the dot.

7 Balance the bird on its beak. Tap its tail gently to make it "peck."

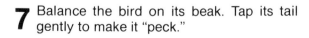

Pig

If all the steps are followed carefully, the finished model will open and close its mouth as you manipulate the paper. To do this, pinch the finished pig by putting your thumbs on the ears and your fingers on the back of the head. Move your hands together and apart.

To make a puppet, omit Step 1 and mount the finished pig on a stick.

Concepts and vocabulary (*See also* page 4)

another
tiny (little)
face
ear
snout
nostrils
pig

Materials

A 6-inch square of thin paper
A pencil, marking pen, or crayon

Additional suggestions

Make the Cat, Dog, and other *Fun Folds* animals. Discuss animal sounds.

How to fold the Pig

1. Put a square of paper on the table so it looks like a diamond.
   Fold the left point over to meet the right point. Unfold.

2. Fold the top point down to meet the bottom point.

3. Now there are two layers. Fold the top layer up a little bit to make a tiny triangle.

4. Fold the little triangle up again to form the snout.

5. Fold the right and left points down to the dots to form ears, as shown. (These ears will cover part of the face.)

6. Fold the bottom point up and tuck it inside.

7. Fold the points of the ears up to the dots, as shown.

8. Draw eyes and nostrils.

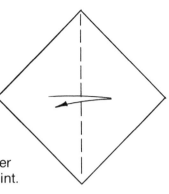

1 Put a square of paper on the table so it looks like a diamond.

Fold the left point over to meet the right point. Unfold.

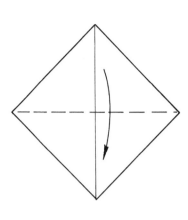

2 Fold the top point down to meet the bottom point.

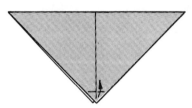

3 Now there are two layers. Fold the top layer up a little bit to make a tiny triangle.

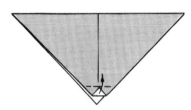

4 Fold the little triangle up again to form the snout.

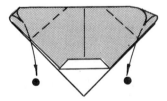

5 Fold the right and left points down to the dots to form ears, as shown. (These ears will cover part of the face.)

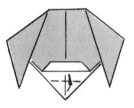

6 Fold the bottom point up and tuck it inside.

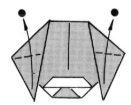

7 Fold the points of the ears up to the dots, as shown.

8 Draw eyes and nostrils.

Rabbit

This model uses the ice-cream cone base that is used for the Swan, Whale, Pecking Bird, Pelican, and other *Fun Folds.*

Concepts and vocabulary (*See also* page 4)

make

cut

bend

teeth

rabbit

eyes

whiskers

Materials

An 8-inch square of thin paper

Scissors

Additional suggestions

Make additional rabbits with ears of varying lengths. (This can be done by adjusting the amount you fold up, in Step 6.) Teach the concept of long, longer, longest.

Make a mask, using a 12-inch square of paper. Cut out the eyes and use string or elastic to hold it in place on the child's face.

How to fold the Rabbit

1. Put a square of paper on the table so it looks like a diamond.
   Fold the left point over to meet the right point. Unfold.

2. Fold the upper left and right sides in to meet the center crease.

3. Fold the top point down to meet the bottom point. Unfold.

4. Cut along the center crease from the top point to the fold you just made.

5. Fold each point down as far as the cut allows.

6. Fold each point up to the dots, as shown.

7. Make a small cut at the bottom, as shown.

8. Fold up the bottom points to make teeth.

9. Fold the points of the teeth down.

10. Turn over. Draw eyes and whiskers. You can bend an ear over, if you like.

1 Put a square of paper on the table so it looks like a diamond.

Fold the left point over to meet the right point. Unfold.

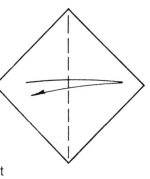

2 Fold the upper left and right sides in to meet the center crease.

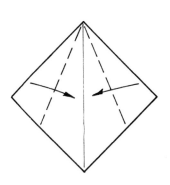

3 Fold the top point down to meet the bottom point. Unfold.

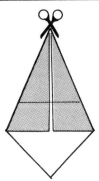

4 Cut along the center crease from the top point to the fold you just made.

5 Fold each point down as far as the cut allows.

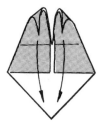

6 Fold each point up to the dots, as shown.

7 Make a small cut at the bottom, as shown.

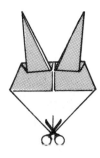

8 Fold up the bottom points to make teeth.

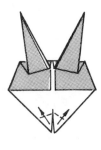

9 Fold the points of the teeth down.

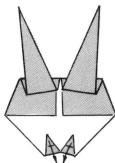

10 Turn over. Draw eyes and whiskers. You can bend an ear over, if you like.

Pelican

Step 6 is a "mountain fold" (see "Symbols").

Step 7 is a preparatory fold. Creasing the paper back and forth makes it easier to push the tail piece through.

If folded carefully, the pelican will stand up.

Concepts and vocabulary (*See also* page 4)
through

middle

reaches

again

tail

piece

pelican

head

tip

place

Materials
A square of thin paper

Additional suggestions
Discuss how pelicans use their long beaks.

Fold the Swan, and compare it to the Pelican. See what other birds can be created from this basic shape.

How to fold the Pelican
1. Put a square of paper on the table so it looks like a diamond.
   Fold the left point over to meet the right point. Unfold.

2. Fold the lower left and right sides to meet the center crease.

3. Again, fold the left and right sides to the center crease.

4. Fold the narrow point up to the wide point. Crease well.

5. Fold the narrow point of the top flap to the bottom to make the head.

6. Pick up the model and fold the sides backward, away from the middle.

7. Fold the tail piece forward, as shown. Crease. Unfold.
   Then fold it backward at the same place. Crease. Unfold.

8. Push the tail piece down and through, using the crease you made in Step 7.

9. Draw eyes.

1 Put a square of paper on the table so it looks like a diamond.

Fold the left point over to meet the right point. Unfold.

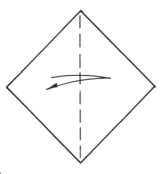

2 Fold the lower left and right sides to meet the center crease.

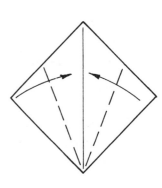

3 Again, fold the left and right sides to the center crease.

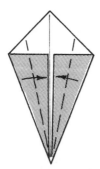

4 Fold the narrow point up to the wide point. Crease well.

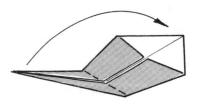

5 Fold the narrow point of the top flap to the bottom to make the head.

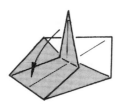

6 Pick up the model and fold the sides backward, away from the middle.

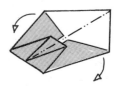

7 Fold the tail piece forward, as shown. Crease. Unfold.

Then fold it backward at the same place. Crease. Unfold.

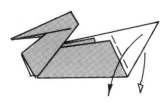

8 Push the tail piece down and through, using the crease you made in Step 7.

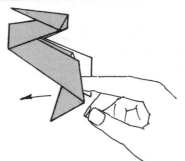

9 Draw eyes.

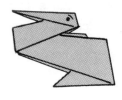

Penguin

This fairly complex model is not suitable for very young children.

Pulling out the head and foot piece is similar to pulling out the legs of the Crab. You may wish to refer to those drawings.

This penguin does not stand up.

Concepts and vocabulary (*See also* page 4)

    reach

    allows

    half

    head

    feet

    penguin

    most

Materials

    A 6-inch or larger square of thin paper, black on one side

    A marking pen

An additional suggestion

    Discuss penguins and other animals that are found in cold climates.

How to fold the Penguin

1. Put a square of paper on the table with the black side up. Turn it so it looks like a diamond. Fold the left point over to meet the right point. Crease. Unfold.

2. Fold the upper left and right sides down to meet the center crease.

3. Fold back the top edges most of the way, as shown.

4. It looks like this.
   Turn over.

5. Fold the bottom point up as far as the paper allows, to make a triangle.

6. Fold the top point down, as shown.

7. Fold in half by bringing the left side over to meet the right side.

8. Reach inside. Pinch and pull out the small triangle at the top. Press flat. This is the penguin's head.
   Repeat with the lower inside piece. This is the penguin's feet.

9. Draw eyes.

1 Put a square of paper on the table with the black side up. Turn it so it looks like a diamond.

Fold the left point over to meet the right point. Crease. Unfold.

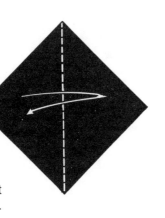

2 Fold the upper left and right sides down to meet the center crease.

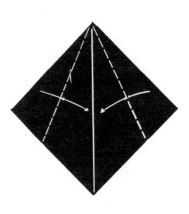

3 Fold back the top edges most of the way, as shown.

4 It looks like this. Turn over.

5 Fold the bottom point up as far as the paper allows, to make a triangle.

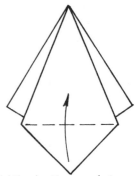

6 Fold the top point down, as shown.

7 Fold in half by bringing the left side over to meet the right side.

8 Reach inside. Pinch and pull out the small triangle at the top. Press flat. This is the penguin's head.

Repeat with the lower inside piece. This is the penguin's feet.

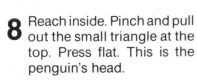

9 Draw eyes.

Seasons

The Lesson Plan Guide

Objectives

To develop auditory and visual attention skills

To develop temporal-spatial concepts

To develop visual-motor skills

To develop auditory and visual sequencing skills

To teach the concepts and vocabulary that are listed for each model in addition to those listed on page 4

Procedure

Give verbal directions as you demonstrate each step.

Follow-up suggestions

See the Language, Social Studies, Science, and Speech Activities related to the Seasons unit (pp. 48-55).

Have the students close their eyes and revisualize each step of the *Fun Folds* as you recount the steps.

Make an experience chart emphasizing the sequential aspects of the lesson.

Have the students teach the *Fun Folds* to others. This activity fosters socialization while emphasizing speech and language development.

Use the *Fun Folds* on the bulletin board or on greeting cards.

Additional suggestions

Additional curriculum-oriented activities are given for individual *Fun Folds.*

Language Activities

These activities develop vocabulary, thinking skills, comprehension, and expression of language. Encourage students to reply in a complete sentence. It may be necessary to repeat the students' answers in expanded sentence form until they begin to respond appropriately.

1. Present, sequence, and classify words that relate to changes in time. Cut out and mount seasonal pictures:

   Seasons

   Months of the year

   Days of the week

   Holidays

   Weather

   Temperature

2. Use the following vocabulary to describe the seasons. Encourage the students to add words to the list and use them in sentences. The students then can draw pictures to illustrate the sentences.

   Adjectives: bright, shiny, misty, clear, early, late, breezy, dark, icy, hot, cold wet, slushy, slippery, chilly, damp, dull, . . .

   Irregular past tense verbs:

cut - cut	wear - wore	draw - drew
eat - ate	light - lit	blow - blew
swim - swam	fall - fell	is - was

   Irregular plural nouns

leaf - leaves	sky - skies

3. Antonyms. Make an antonym tree with the students. Words can be printed and mounted on leaves, apples, and so on.

Spring - Fall	land - sea	warm - cool
Winter - Summer	first - last	sunny - rainy
work - vacation	hot - cold	cloudy - clear
before - after	sunrise - sunset	windy - calm

4. Synonyms. Write synonyms on *Fun Folds* snowflakes.

first - beginning	last - end	work - job
sunrise - dawn	sunset - dusk	vacation - rest

5. Homographs. The students can illustrate and write sentences that show the multiple meanings of words (for example, The bicycle seat spring is broken, The weather is warm in the Spring).

blue	stamp	light
cold	fly	last
change	season	march
plant	hatch	may
fall	wave	

6. Homonyms. Have the students draw pictures or write sentences that show meanings of homonyms.

weather - whether	blew - blue
rain - rein - reign	sun - son

7. Similarities and differences. Have the students explain how these seasonal words are the same and how they are different:

Halloween - Thanksgiving	July - December
winter - summer	spring - fall
Thursday - Sunday	cold - hot
baseball - football	ice skates - sled
valentines - cards	mittens - gloves
pumpkin - turkey	week - month

8. Categories. This activity develops auditory memory, comprehension, and oral language skills. Have the students repeat each group of words after you. Ask them which word does not belong. Have them explain their choices. (Note: For younger students, use picture cards to augment oral presentation.)

   hot - cold - Monday - warm

   Monday - January - Thursday - Friday

   October - December - Tuesday - May

   sunny - Halloween - Christmas - Thanksgiving

   June - rainy - sunny - snowy

   football - baseball - soccer - pumpkin

   turkey - ice skates - sled - snowman

   winter - spring - Wednesday - summer

   mittens - swimsuit - scarf - coat

9. Auditory closure. This activity develops vocabulary, thinking skills, verbal expression, and oral language structure. Review holidays, seasons, weather, and temperature. Then have the students listen as you read the sentences. Ask them to supply the missing word. Explain that in each group, we are listening for a holiday, a season, weather, or temperature.

   Holidays:

   We carve a jack-o'-lantern for _____ . (Halloween)

   We draw hearts for _____ . (Valentine's Day)

   We prepare a feast for _____ . (Thanksgiving)

   We vote on _____ . (Election Day)

   We see fireworks displayed on the _____ . (Fourth of July)

   We decorate a tree for _____ . (Christmas)

   We light candles for _____ . (Hanukkah)

   In February we celebrate the birthdays of _____ . (Washington, Lincoln)

   We march in a parade on _____ . (Memorial Day)

   We dye eggs for _____ . (Easter)

   Seasons:

   We build a snowman in the _____ . (winter)

   We rake leaves in the _____ . (fall)

   We swim in the _____ . (summer)

   We plant seeds in the _____ . (spring)

   We shovel snow in the _____ . (winter)

   We sail in the _____ . (summer)

   We play baseball in the _____ . (spring)

   We play football in the _____ . (fall)

   We build an igloo in the _____ . (winter)

Weather and temperature:

We wear boots when it _____ . (rains, snows)

We wear a swimsuit when it is _____ . (hot)

We wear mittens when it is _____ . (cold)

We wear a sweater when it is _____ . (cool)

We use an umbrella when it _____ . (rains)

10. Analogies. This activity develops auditory attention skills, auditory association, auditory closure, and oral expression. It also can be presented as a written exercise to develop visual closure skills. Read the following analogies aloud, emphasizing the key word in each analogy. This will help the students to focus more clearly on the correct solution.

Jack-o'-lantern is to **Halloween** as turkey is to _____ . (Thanksgiving)

Leaves are to **fall** as buds are to _____ . (spring)

Snow is to **winter** as flowers are to _____ . (summer)

Hearts are to **Valentine's Day** as ballots are to _____ . (Election Day)

Monday is to **week** as November is to _____ . (year)

Cold is to **temperature** as sunny is to _____ . (weather)

Fall is to **football** as spring is to _____ . (baseball)

Days are to **week** as months are to _____ . (year)

Hot is to **summer** as cold is to _____ . (winter)

11. Sequence activities. Prepare duplicate sets of index cards with pictures or words of the days of the week, months of the year, seasons, and holidays. Divide them into decks of cards.

Play "Concentration."

Play "Months of the Year," "Seasons," and "Days of the Week" card games. After all cards have been matched or paired, have the students sequence them appropriately.

Mix month and holiday cards. Have the students match holiday cards to month cards. When all matches are complete, have the students sequence them appropriately.

12. Crossword puzzle and word scramble. This activity develops visual sequencing, visual memory, and visual-motor skills. Reproduce and distribute the worksheet on the following page.

Answer key: DOWN—fall, winter, rain, spring, snow, melt, fog

ACROSS—flower, ants, plant, nest, summer, ski, leaf, bug

"Seasons" Worksheet

Name _____ Date _____

Directions: Unscramble the "Seasons" words.
Then, using the letter clues, fill in the Flower Crossword Puzzle.

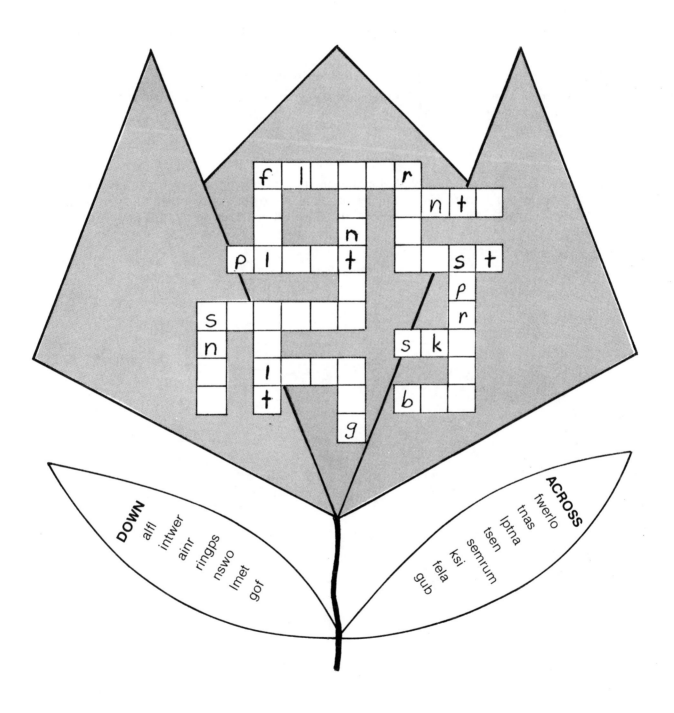

DOWN
alfl
intwer
ainr
ringps
nswo
lmet
gof

ACROSS
fwerlo
tnas
lptna
tsen
semrum
ksi
fela
gub

Social Studies Activities

Election Day: Familiarize the students with the meaning of these words: ballot, laws, committee, judge, court, jail, crime, innocent, guilty, defendant.

Hold a class election and have students vote by secret ballot.

Dramatize a courtroom proceeding. Have students assume the roles of judge, defendant, and others.

Set up a committee to plan a holiday party or other class function.

Winter Festival: Have the students research holiday customs throughout the community, the country, and the world. Plan a holiday celebration, with activities that reflect different cultures and customs.

Valentine's Day: Have the students make valentines for each other.

Set up a mailbox and post office center. Teach the concept of mail, postage, address, return address, zip code, deliver, and so on.

Choose students to "sell" stamps.

Choose students to deliver the mail.

Presidents' Day: Discuss the lives of Washington and Lincoln. Compare their home environment, education, form of transportation, and leisure activities to our own. Prepare a play or skit that recreates their way of life. List the differences between these Presidents' lives and our own on a chart.

Sample chart:

	President	Us
Home		
Play		
School		
Work		
Transportation		

Science Activities

1. Prepare a bulletin board showing changes in the temperature, weather, and activities as the seasons change.

2. Discuss the sports we participate in during fall, winter, spring, and summer.

3. Discuss the clothing we wear each season.

4. Discuss chores associated with the seasons (raking leaves in the fall, shoveling snow in the winter, planting a garden in the spring, watering the grass and mowing the lawn in summer).

5. Illustrate the saying "March comes in like a lion and goes out like a lamb."
   Discuss the change in weather from winter to spring.

6. Discuss changes in animal behavior from one season to another.
   Discuss the habits of squirrels and the hibernation of bears.

7. Discuss various holidays and the season in which they occur.

8. Halloween activities:
   a. Visit a pumpkin farm.
   b. Discuss how pumpkins grow.
   c. Discuss plant nutrition.
   d. Carve a jack-o'-lantern with the students.
   e. Bake pumpkin seeds.
   f. Discuss the multiple uses of plants.
   g. Prepare a chart that shows various foods in raw and processed stages (for example, pumpkin - pumpkin pie).

9. Thanksgiving activities:
   a. Discuss the Pilgrims' means of transportation to the New World. Compare and contrast it to present, more rapid means of transportation.
   b. Riddle: What has an ear and cannot hear? (An ear of corn.) Examine and name the parts of an ear of corn (husk, cob, kernel).
   c. Plant a kernel of popcorn. Chart its growth.
      (1) Place a paper towel in a glass. Put soil in the glass. Put popcorn seeds between the glass and the paper towel. Water the soil, making sure the paper towel gets wet. Set the glass in the sun.
      (2) When the paper towel becomes dry, put more water in the glass.
          Soon the roots will grow. Later, the corn plants will appear and grow.
   d. Make popcorn with the class. Discuss the process that occurs when heat causes the kernels to expand and pop.

10. Winter activities:

   a. Discuss the use of candles for various winter holidays such as Christmas and Hanukkah.

   b. Light a candle with the class. Observe the wax melt as the candle burns.

   c. Compare the candle with other sources of light (flashlight, electric light, sunlight).

   d. Discuss heat as a form of energy.

   e. (1) Place a pan of water on a window ledge on a day when the temperature is freezing. Have the students note the change from liquid to solid state.

   (2) Bring the pan of water indoors. Have the students note the effect of the warm temperature on the frozen water.

11. Spring activities:

   a. Discuss windpower.

   b. Fly *Fun Folds* kites and planes. Note changes when the kites and planes are flown indoors and outdoors. (See the sample bar graph in "Transportation: Science Activities.")

   c. Discuss changes in animal habits. Discuss awakening of the bear from hibernation.

   d. Plant seeds with the students. Chart their growth. Discuss what the seeds need to help them grow. Discuss the best growing environment.

   e. Prepare an incubator in the classroom, and watch an egg hatch. Keep a log to note daily changes.

   f. Take a walking tour of the environment surrounding the school. Look for signs of spring.

12. Other activities with charts and graphs:

   a. Teach and compare Fahrenheit and centigrade.

   b. Prepare a temperature chart each week.

   c. Save the weekly temperature charts. Compare temperature changes between months, seasons, years.

   d. Each week, appoint a student to be the weather person, who will give the class a daily weather report.

   e. Prepare a bar graph showing how many days there are in each month. Discuss the longest and shortest months.

   f. Teach the concept of leap year.

   g. Record birthdays each month. Note which month has the most and the least birthdays.

Speech Activities

The following are excellent as carryover activities for articulation therapy, voice therapy, and fluency practice.

1. Have students teach the "Seasons" *Fun Folds* to others. This activity provides an opportunity for students to practice tension-free vocal quality and improve pitch, volume, and rate. Children who stutter can build confidence as they practice fluent speech.

2. Display posters showing seasonal activities. Have students locate and name activities that contain their speech sound. For example:

   /s/: The boy is ice skating.　　　　　/r/: The boy is raking leaves.

   　　　The girl is skiing.　　　　　　　　　The leaves are red and orange.

3. Mount seasonal pictures on construction paper. Then mount pictures of seasonal items containing target sounds (leaves, rowboat, sled, etc.) on small squares of paper. Prop up the seasonal pictures. Select a picture of an item containing the target sound, and hide it behind one of the seasonal pictures. Have the students guess the item's location ("Is the rake behind the fall picture?"). The student who guesses correctly takes the next turn.

Tulip

This fold is suitable for very young children. It can be taught using the terms "one side" and "the other side" instead of "right side" and "left side." To further simplify this model, use a triangle and begin with Step 2.

Concepts and vocabulary (*See also* page 4)

add

stem

leaves

tulip

Material

A small square of thin paper. If heavier paper is used, staple the final step.

Additional suggestions

Make colorful tulips for a springtime exhibit.

Discuss other signs of spring.

Make a tulip, and paste it on a piece of construction paper. Draw and label the stem, leaves, and petals.

How to fold the Tulip

1. Put a square of paper on the table so it looks like a diamond.
   Fold the bottom point up to meet the top point.

2. Fold the right point up beside the top point to the dot, as shown.

3. Fold the left point up beside the top point to the dot, as shown.

4. The tulip

5. Add a stem and some leaves.

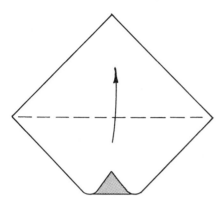

1 Put a square of paper on the table so it looks like a diamond.

Fold the bottom point up to meet the top point.

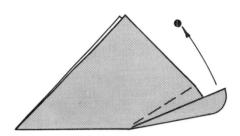

2 Fold the right point up beside the top point to the dot, as shown.

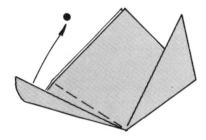

3 Fold the left point up beside the top point to the dot, as shown.

4 The tulip

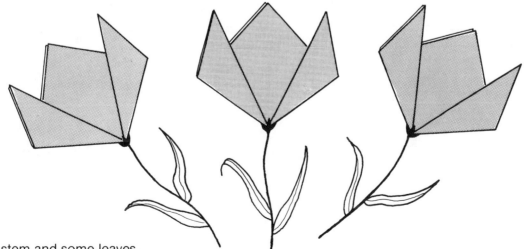

5 Add a stem and some leaves.

Heart

Concepts and vocabulary (*See also* page 4)

find

house

heart

Materials

A rectangle of thin paper, 8½ inches by 2½ inches (use the strip that remains after you cut an 8½-inch square from an 8½-inch by 11-inch rectangle of paper)

Additional suggestions

Make this model for Valentine's Day. Open it to write a message.

Make several hearts with progressively smaller rectangles. Glue them together, according to size. Teach the concept of small, smaller, smallest.

For St. Patrick's Day, make three green hearts to form a shamrock. Add a stem.

Turn over the "tent" at Step 4, to make a house. Make three pig puppets and a wolf puppet to "huff and puff and blow the house down" in a dramatization of *The Three Little Pigs.*

How to fold the Heart

1. Put a rectangle of paper on the table with the long edges at the top and bottom.
   Fold the left side over to meet the right side. Unfold.

2. Fold the top left edge down to meet the center crease.

3. Fold the top right edge down to meet the center crease.

4. It looks like a tent. Turn over.

5. Now it looks like a house.

6. Turn the top around to the bottom. Find four corners at the top. Fold each corner down into a small triangle.

7. Now it looks like this. Turn over.

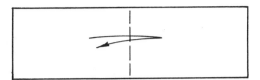

1 Put a rectangle of paper on the table with the long edges at the top and bottom.

Fold the left side over to meet the right side. Unfold.

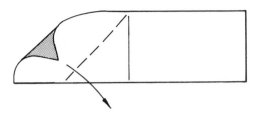

2 Fold the top left edge down to meet the center crease.

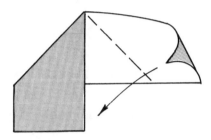

3 Fold the top right edge down to meet the center crease.

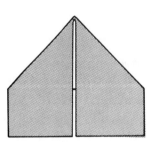

4 It looks like a tent. Turn over.

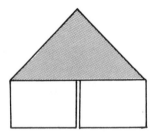

5 Now it looks like a house.

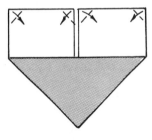

6 Turn the top around to the bottom. Find four corners at the top. Fold each corner down into a small triangle.

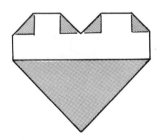

7 Now it looks like this. Turn over.

Flag

This model is suitable for very young children.

Concepts and vocabulary (*See also* page 4)

begin

again

another

pole

flag

Materials

A sheet of notebook or duplicating paper

Scissors

Stapler

Additional suggestions

Children with good small muscle control can make another flag with the piece that was cut away. The procedure can be repeated again and again until the paper is too small to work with.

Have the students decorate their flags and have a classroom parade to marching music.

Teach the concepts of halves and quarters.

How to fold the Flag

1. Put a rectangle of paper on the table with the long edges at the top and bottom. Fold the bottom edge to the top. Crease. Unfold.

2. Fold the left short side over to meet the right short side. Crease. Unfold.

3. Cut away one of the sections, as shown.

4. It looks like this.

5. Fold the left side over to begin forming a pole, as shown.

6. Fold the left folded side over again.

7. Staple it closed, as shown.

8. Now make another flag with the rectangle you cut away in Step 3.

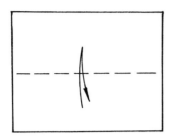

1 Put a rectangle of paper on the table with the long edges at the top and bottom. Fold the bottom edge to the top. Crease. Unfold.

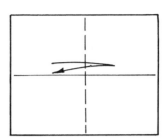

2 Fold the left short side over to meet the right short side. Crease. Unfold.

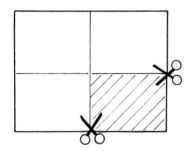

3 Cut away one of the sections, as shown.

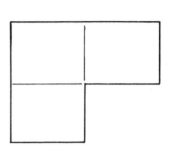

4 It looks like this.

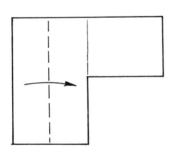

5 Fold the left side over to begin forming a pole, as shown.

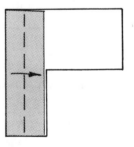

6 Fold the left folded side over again.

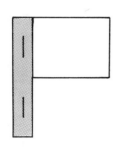

7 Staple it closed, as shown.

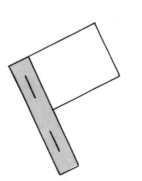

8 Now make another flag with the rectangle you cut away in Step 3.

Halloween Masks

Although these masks appear to be simple, cutting out the features may be difficult for young children.

Concepts and vocabulary (*See also* page 4)

> attach
>
> glue
>
> design
>
> yarn
>
> witch
>
> clown
>
> face
>
> mask

Materials

> A 12-inch or larger square of paper
>
> Glue
>
> Paper punch
>
> Yarn
>
> Crayons or marking pens
>
> Scissors

Additional suggestions

> Draw features on the face of the mask. Discuss parts of the face.
>
> Make happy and sad face masks. Discuss emotions.
>
> Many *Fun Folds* in the Animals unit make suitable masks.

How to fold Halloween Masks

1. Put a square of paper on the table so it looks like a diamond.
   Fold the left point over to meet the right point. Crease. Unfold.

2. Bring the upper left side down to meet the center crease.

3. Repeat with the upper right side.

4. Glue down the long triangles. Punch a hole at each side. Attach yarn

5. Draw and cut out faces.
   Design your mask.

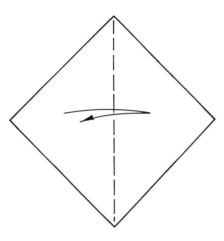

1 Put a square of paper on the table so it looks like a diamond.

Fold the left point over to meet the right point. Crease. Unfold.

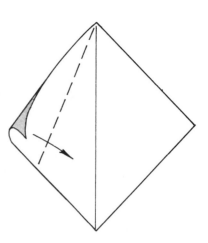

2 Bring the upper left side down to meet the center crease.

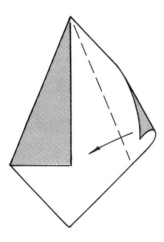

3 Repeat with the upper right side.

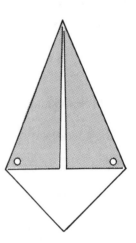

4 Glue down the long triangles. Punch a hole at each side. Attach yarn

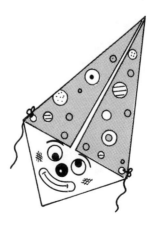

5 Draw and cut out faces.
Design your mask.

New Year's Hat

This fold is suitable for very young children. It can be taught using the terms "one side" and "the other side" instead of "right side" and "left side."

Concepts and vocabulary (*See also* page 4)

New Year

Materials

A 20-inch square of newsprint, gift wrap, or other thin paper. If heavier paper is used, staple the final step.

Additional suggestions

The hat may be decorated with crayons or markers, stickers, and so on.

Make another model using an 8½-inch square of clean paper. Turn it upside down and use it for a drinking cup.

How to fold a New Year's Hat

1. Put a square of paper on the table so it looks like a diamond.
   Fold the top point down to meet the bottom point.

2. Fold the left point over to the dot.

3. Fold the right point over to the other dot.

4. The triangle at the bottom has two layers. Lift up the top layer as far as it will go.

5. Turn over. Repeat on the other side.

6. Happy New Year!

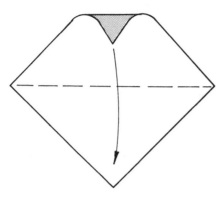

1 Put a square of paper on the table so it looks like a diamond.

Fold the top point down to meet the bottom point.

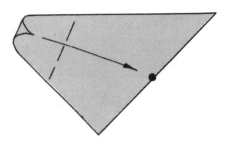

2 Fold the left point over to the dot.

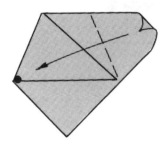

3 Fold the right point over to the other dot.

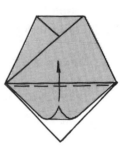

4 The triangle at the bottom has two layers. Lift up the top layer as far as it will go.

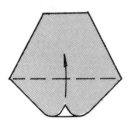

5 Turn over. Repeat on the other side.

6 Happy New Year!

May Basket

Be careful at Step 6. The cut is made parallel to the slanted edge. No paper is cut away. You may wish to have the students draw this line before the cut is made.

Concepts and vocabulary (*See also* page 4)
> basket
>
> along

Materials
> Use any square of paper. If it is very thick (for example, wallpaper), staples may be needed.
> Scissors
> A pencil

Additional suggestions
> For Halloween, make a large basket for use as a "trick or treat" bag.
> Hang baskets on the Christmas tree, and fill with candy.
> Make the Flower or the Tulip to put in the basket for Mother's Day.

How to fold the May Basket

1. Put a square of paper on the table so it looks like a diamond.
   Fold the bottom point up to meet the top point.

2. Fold the bottom left corner over to the dot, as shown.

3. Fold the bottom right corner over to the dot, as shown.

4. It looks like this.

5. Fold the left folded edge over to meet the right edge.

6. Cut along the line to the dot. Do *not* cut to the edge. Unfold.

7. Fold down the top layer only of the small cut triangle.

8. Turn over. Repeat on the other side.

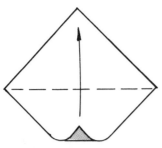

1 Put a square of paper on the table so it looks like a diamond.
Fold the bottom point up to meet the top point.

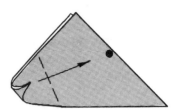

2 Fold the bottom left corner over to the dot, as shown.

3 Fold the bottom right corner over to the dot, as shown.

4 It looks like this.

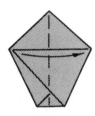

5 Fold the left folded edge over to meet the right edge.

6 Cut along the line to the dot. Do *not* cut to the edge. Unfold.

7 Fold down the top layer only of the small cut triangle.

8 Turn over. Repeat on the other side.

Kite

Make and fly this kite on a windy March day!

Concepts and vocabulary (*See also* page 4)

punch

string

tail

kite

reinforce

hole

tie

only

Materials

A 10-inch square of colorful paper

Paper punch

Kite string

6-inch by ½-inch strips of crepe paper for the tail

Additional suggestions

Discuss other things that fly: birds, butterflies, planes, rocket ships. Make those *Fun Folds* models.

Teach the multiple meanings of the words *tie* and *punch*.

Teach the homographs *tail-tale, hole-whole.*

How to fold the Kite

1. Put a square of paper on the table so it looks like a diamond.
   Fold the left point to meet the right point.

2. Unfold. Turn over.

3. Fold the left upper side down to the center crease.

4. Repeat with the right upper side.

5. Fold the center points outward to the folded sides, as shown.

6. Punch holes at the three dots, as shown. (Be careful to punch holes through only one layer.) Reinforce the holes.

7. Attach a long piece of string, as shown. Attach a short piece of string for the tail. Tie strips of crepe paper on the tail.

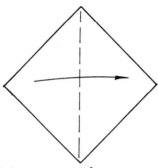

1 Put a square of paper on the table so it looks like a diamond.

Fold the left point to meet the right point.

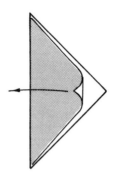

2 Unfold. Turn over.

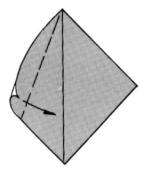

3 Fold the left upper side down to the center crease.

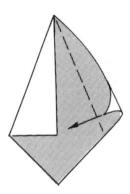

4 Repeat with the right upper side.

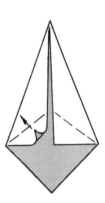

5 Fold the center points outward to the folded sides, as shown.

6 Punch holes at the three dots, as shown. (Be careful to punch holes through only one layer.) Reinforce the holes.

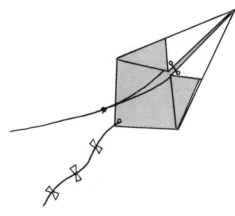

7 Attach a long piece of string, as shown. Attach a short piece of string for the tail. Tie strips of crepe paper on the tail.

Fan

Hints

The fan folds should be between ½-inch and ¾-inch wide.

Another way to "fan fold" is to pull the short edge of the paper toward you, using the table edge as a guide. With this method, it is not necessary to turn the paper over between each step.

Concepts and vocabulary (*See also* page 4)

closed

continue

reach

staple

handle

thumb

Materials

A 10-inch by 5-inch rectangle, or any rectangle with one side twice as long as the other

Stapler

Scissors (for circular fan)

A handle (for circular fan)

Additional suggestions

Design your own fan by decorating the paper before you fold.

Attach a fan to the back of a *Fun Folds* Swan to make a peacock.

Compare the paper fan to other cooling devices (air conditioner, electric fan).

How to fold the Fan

1. Put a rectangle of paper on the table with the short edges at the top and bottom.
   Fold up a small piece (about as wide as your thumb) from the bottom.

2. Turn over. Fold up again.

3. It looks like this.
   Turn over.

4. Fold up the folded edge again.

5. It looks like this.
   Turn over again.

6. It looks like this.
   Now fold up the folded edge again.

7. Continue to turn over and fold up until you reach the top edge.

8. Staple the fan closed at the bottom, to make a handle.

9. For a circular fan, staple in the middle and cut off the points, as shown.
   Staple or tape the ends into a circle.
   Add a handle.

1 Put a rectangle of paper on the table with the short edges at the top and bottom.

Fold up a small piece (about as wide as your thumb) from the bottom.

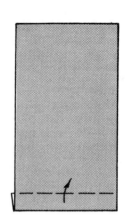

2 Turn over. Fold up again.

3 It looks like this. Turn over.

4 Fold up the folded edge again.

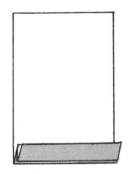

5 It looks like this. Turn over again.

6 It looks like this.

Now fold up the folded edge again.

7 Continue to turn over and fold up until you reach the top edge.

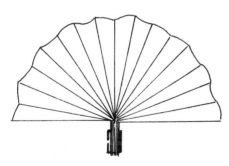

8 Staple the fan closed at the bottom, to make a handle.

9 For a circular fan, staple in the middle and cut off the points, as shown.

Staple or tape the ends into a circle.

Add a handle.

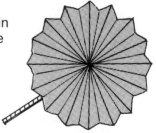

Candy Cane

Hints

Young children may find it difficult to roll the paper as shown in Step 4. It may be helpful to have them roll it tightly over a pencil.

Paper-backed foil gift wrap is ideal for this fold. Plain white paper can be used, however. Color the letter L instead of folding it as it appears in step 3

Concepts and vocabulary (*See also* page 4)

starting

letter L

curl

candy cane

form

hold

hook

Materials

A square of paper colored on one side

Tape or glue

Additional suggestions

Make several candy canes to hang on the Christmas tree or to decorate holiday gifts.

Discuss the multiple meanings of the word cane (sugar, candy, and aid for the handicapped).

How to fold the Candy Cane

1. Put a square of paper on the table. Begin with the white side up.
   Fold the left side in a little bit.

2. Fold the bottom edge up a little bit to form the letter L.

3. Hold the top right corner (on the white side), and turn the paper over. *Don't let go!*

4. Roll the corner you are holding to the opposite corner.

5. Glue or tape the point so the cane is closed.
   Press the top half flat.
   Curl it over to form a hook.

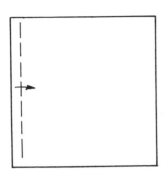

1 Put a square of paper on the table. Begin with the white side up.

Fold the left side in a little bit.

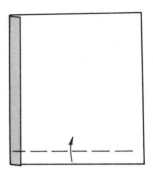

2 Fold the bottom edge up a little bit to form the letter L.

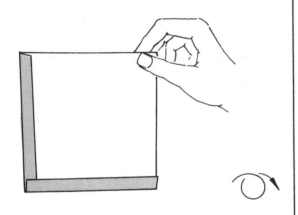

3 Hold the top right corner (on the white side), and turn the paper over. *Don't let go!*

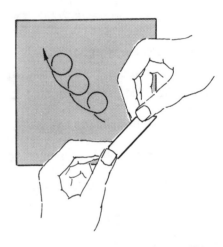

4 Roll the corner you are holding to the opposite corner.

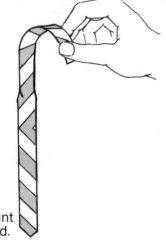

5 Glue or tape the point so the cane is closed.

Press the top half flat.

Curl it over to form a hook.

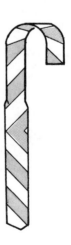

Notebook

This model is suitable for young children. Only the final assembly is a bit tricky.

Concepts and vocabulary (*See also* page 4)

together

stand

again

notebook

Materials

A sheet of notebook or duplicating paper

Scissors

Additional suggestions

Use the finished model for a homework assignment notebook.

Make an invitation to "Back to School Night," using this model.

Teach the concepts of halves, quarters, and eighths.

How to fold the Notebook

1. Put a rectangle of paper on the table with the long edges at the top and the bottom. Fold the bottom edge up to meet the top. Crease. Unfold.

2. Fold the left side over to meet the right side. Do not unfold.

3. Fold the left folded side over to meet the right side.

4. Unfold the last fold you made.

5. Cut along the center line from the folded side to the midpoint only.

6. Unfold.

7. Fold the top edge down to the bottom again.

8. Stand the paper up. Push together to form a book, using the folds you have made.

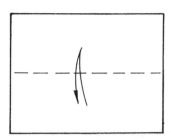

1 Put a rectangle of paper on the table with the long edges at the top and the bottom.

Fold the bottom edge up to meet the top. Crease. Unfold.

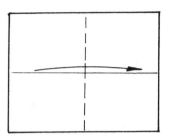

2 Fold the left side over to meet the right side. Do not unfold.

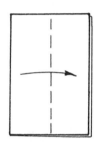

3 Fold the left folded side over to meet the right side.

4 Unfold the last fold you made.

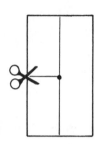

5 Cut along the center line from the folded side to the midpoint only.

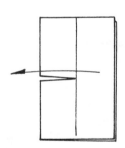

6 Unfold.

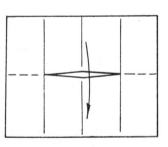

7 Fold the top edge down to the bottom again.

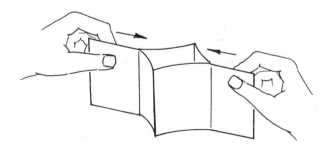

8 Stand the paper up. Push together to form a book, using the folds you have made.

Picture Frame

This model requires accuracy in folding. It is not suitable for very young children.

Hints

A 6-inch square of paper fits a 3-inch picture.

Foil-backed gift wrap is most suitable for this model.

Step 4 may present some difficulty, since the students do not have crease lines to guide them.

Concepts and vocabulary (*See also* page 4)

again

starting

each

stand

picture frame

Materials

A 6-inch or larger square of paper, colored on one side

Additional suggestions

Draw a picture to put into the frame for a gift for Valentine's Day, Mother's or Father's Day, or other occasion.

Draw happy and sad faces to put in the picture frame. Discuss emotions.

Use this model to teach concepts of halves and quarters.

Discuss different types of frames (door, window, picture).

How to fold the Picture Frame

1. Put a square of paper on the table with the colored side facing you.
   Fold the bottom edge up to the top. Crease. Unfold.
   Fold the left side to the right side. Crease. Unfold.

2. Fold each corner to the midpoint.

3. It looks like this.
   Turn over.

4. Fold each corner to the midpoint again.

5. Now it looks like this.
   Turn over again.

6. Starting at the midpoint, fold each inside corner to the outside corner, forming small triangles.

7. Turn the picture frame over.

8. Make a stand by pulling down one corner on the back.

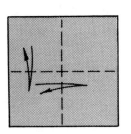

1 Put a square of paper on the table with the colored side facing you.

Fold the bottom edge up to the top. Crease. Unfold.

Fold the left side to the right side. Crease. Unfold.

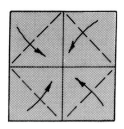

2 Fold each corner to the midpoint.

3 It looks like this. Turn over.

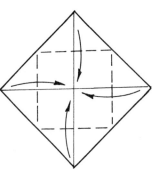

4 Fold each corner to the midpoint again.

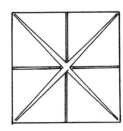

5 Now it looks like this. Turn over again.

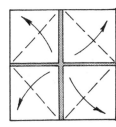

6 Starting at the midpoint, fold each inside corner to the outside corner, forming small triangles.

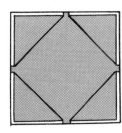

7 Turn the picture frame over.

8 Make a stand by pulling down one corner on the back.

"Candle-Folded" Napkin

This model is not suitable for young children. It is difficult to keep a straight edge as you roll up the napkin.

Concepts and vocabulary (*See also* page 4)

smaller

bigger

continue

band

end

roll

straight

candle

inches

Materials

A square paper or cloth napkin

Additional suggestions

Discuss measurements. Look for things that measure about two inches.
Use this fold for a table setting for a party or snack.

How to fold the "Candle-Folded" Napkin

1. Unfold the napkin and put it on the table so it looks like a diamond.
   Fold the bottom point up to meet the top point.

2. Fold up the bottom folded edge a little bit to make a band.

3. It looks like a boat.
   Turn over and put it down with the folded edge on the right.

4. Begin at the bottom point and roll upward. Be sure to keep the right folded edge straight.

5. Continue rolling. Stop about two inches from the top.

6. Tuck the end point into the band.
   See if your "candle" will stand.

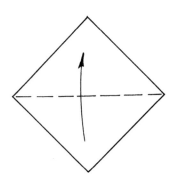

1 Unfold the napkin and put it on the table so it looks like a diamond.

Fold the bottom point up to meet the top point.

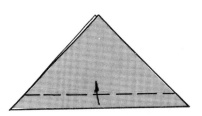

2 Fold up the bottom folded edge a little bit to make a band.

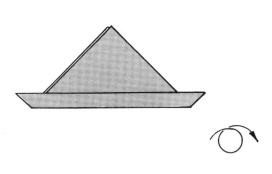

3 It looks like a boat.

Turn over and put it down with the folded edge on the right.

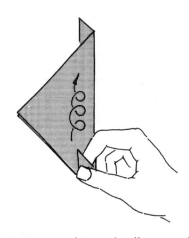

4 Begin at the bottom point and roll upward. Be sure to keep the right folded edge straight.

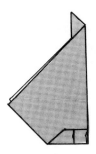

5 Continue rolling. Stop about two inches from the top.

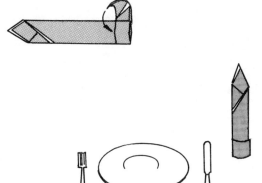

6 Tuck the end point into the band.

See if your "candle" will stand.

Butterfly

This model is rather difficult for children because it requires fan-folding on the diagonal. Make the Fan before attempting the Butterfly.

Hint

If the children are familiar with fan-folding, you can omit the first eight steps and just fan-fold on the diagonal, then continue with Step 9.

Concepts and vocabulary (*See also* page 4)

smaller	diagrams
bigger	entire
continue	finally
piece	butterfly
next	pipe cleaner

Materials

A 10-inch square of thin paper
A 6-inch square of thin paper
A pipe cleaner or twist-tie

Additional suggestions

Make a mobile, using several *Fun Folds* butterflies.
Discuss where butterflies come from. Discuss egg masses, caterpillars, and cocoons.

How to fold the Butterfly

1. Put the larger square of paper on the table so it looks like a diamond.
   Fold the bottom point up to meet the top point. Crease. Unfold.

2. Fold the bottom point up to the center crease. Then fold the point down to the bottom.

3. Fold the point up to the folded edge.

4. Unfold as shown.

5. Fold the bottom edge up to that crease.

6. It looks like this.
   Turn over.

7. Fold up along that crease and continue to turn over and fold up toward the opposite point.

8. It looks like this.
   Continue folding until the entire paper is folded like a fan.

9. It looks like this.

10. Make another fan-fold with the smaller square of paper. Put that piece on top of the larger one. Twist closed with a twist-tie or pipe cleaner.

11. Spread the wings apart.

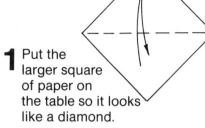

1 Put the larger square of paper on the table so it looks like a diamond.
Fold the bottom point up to meet the top point. Crease. Unfold.

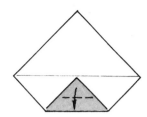

2 Fold the bottom point up to the center crease. Then fold the point down to the bottom.

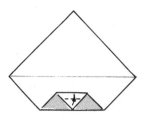

3 Fold the point up to the folded edge.

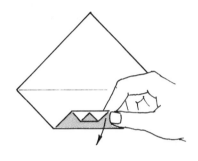

4 Unfold as shown.

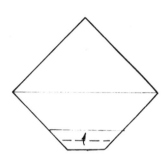

5 Fold the bottom edge up to that crease.

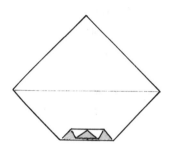

6 It looks like this. Turn over.

7 Fold up along that crease and continue to turn over and fold up toward the opposite point.

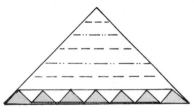

8 It looks like this.
Continue folding until the entire paper is folded like a fan.

9 It looks like this.

10 Make another fan-fold with the smaller square of paper. Put that piece on top of the larger one. Twist closed with a twist-tie or pipe cleaner.

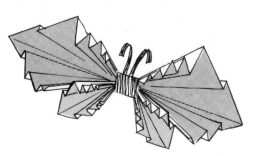

11 Spread the wings apart.

Snowflake

This fairly complex model is not suitable for very young children.

Hint

Because this model is folded into many layers, use very thin paper, such as tissue paper.

Concepts and vocabulary (*See also* page 4)

through

wherever

careful

discard

across

half

wish

snowflake

Materials

A square of very thin paper

Scissors

An additional suggestion

Compare finished snowflakes. Note that no two are alike. Discuss the concept of individuality.

How to fold the Snowflake

1. Put a square of thin paper on the table so it looks like a diamond.
   Fold the bottom point up to meet the top point.

2. Fold the left point over to meet the right point. Crease. Unfold.

3. Fold the left point over to the dot, as shown.

4. Fold the right point over to the dot, as shown.
   Push and pull until the outer edges line up.

5. Fold in half. Crease well.

6. Cut from dot to dot through all layers, as shown. Discard the top piece.

7. Cut out little triangle shapes wherever you wish. Be careful not to cut all the way across the paper.

8. Open.

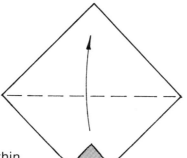

1 Put a square of thin paper on the table so it looks like a diamond.

Fold the bottom point up to meet the top point.

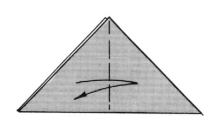

2 Fold the left point over to meet the right point. Crease. Unfold.

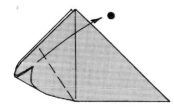

3 Fold the left point over to the dot, as shown.

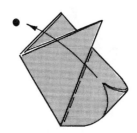

4 Fold the right point over to the dot, as shown. Push and pull until the outer edges line up.

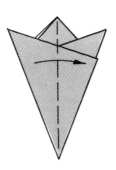

5 Fold in half. Crease well.

6 Cut from dot to dot through all layers, as shown. Discard the top piece.

7 Cut out little triangle shapes wherever you wish. Be careful not to cut all the way across the paper.

8 Open.

Flower

This complex model is not suitable for very young children.

Hints

Read Steps 1 and 2 carefully. When you "push together and flatten" in Step 3, be sure the shape looks like a square with two flaps on each side. This square base is used for many advanced paper-folded creations.

If paper is colored on one side, begin with the colored side facing you. Additional flowers can be begun with the white side facing you.

Concepts and vocabulary (*See also* page 4)

flatten

together

hold

petal

stem

pipe cleaner

flower

Materials

A 6-inch square of thin paper

Scissors

Pipe cleaners

Additional suggestions

Make the May Basket. Fill it with these flowers for a Mother's Day gift.

Use this model to teach halves, quarters, and eighths.

How to fold the Flower

1. Put a square of paper on the table so it looks like a diamond.

    Fold the left point over to meet the right point. Crease. Unfold.

    Fold the bottom point up to meet the top. Crease. Unfold.

2. Turn over. Put the paper on the table as a square.

    Fold the left side over to meet the right side. Crease. Unfold.

    Fold the bottom edge up to meet the top. Do not unfold.

3. Hold along the bottom folded edge. Push the four corners together. Press flat.

4. The little diamond shape has two flaps on each side. Using the top layers only, fold the right and left folded sides in to meet the center crease.

5. Turn over. Repeat Step 4 on the back.

6. Cut out little points at the top edges.

7. Fold down the top layer only, as shown. Flatten the side petals.

8. Add pipe cleaners to make stems.

1 Put a square of paper on the table so it looks like a diamond.

Fold the left point over to meet the right point. Crease. Unfold.

Fold the bottom point up to meet the top. Crease. Unfold.

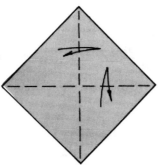

2 Turn over. Put the paper on the table as a square.

Fold the left side over to meet the right side. Crease. Unfold.

Fold the bottom edge up to meet the top. Do not unfold.

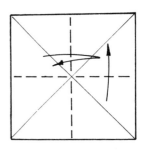

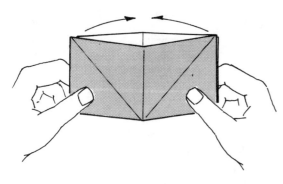

3 Hold along the bottom folded edge. Push the four corners together. Press flat.

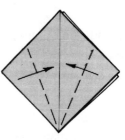

4 The little diamond shape has two flaps on each side. Using the top layers only, fold the right and left folded sides in to meet the center crease.

5 Turn over. Repeat Step 4 on the back.

6 Cut out little points at the top edges.

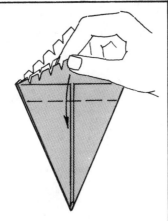

7 Fold down the top layer only, as shown. Flatten the side petals.

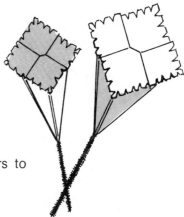

8 Add pipe cleaners to make stems.

Colonial Bonnet

Hints

This is a complex model. Read Steps 1 through 3 carefully. When you push together and flatten, be sure the shape ends up looking like a triangle with two flaps on each side. This triangular base is used for many advanced paper-folded creations.

Step 7 can be done more easily if the points are folded down and taped, rather than tucked in.

Concepts and vocabulary (*See also* page 4)

pinch	loose
together	far
piece	carefully
bend	bonnet

Materials

A large square of thin paper

Paper punch

Ribbons or yarn

Additional suggestions

The students may wear the Bonnet at a Thanksgiving feast or play.

Use this model to teach the concepts of halves, quarters, and eighths.

Discuss different head coverings (football helmet, baseball hat, and so on).

How to fold the Colonial Bonnet

1. Fold the bottom edge of the square up to meet the top edge. Crease. Unfold.
    Fold the left side over to meet the right side. Crease. Unfold.

2. Turn over. Put it on the table so it looks like a diamond.
    Fold the left point over to meet the right point. Crease. Unfold.
    Fold the top point down to meet the bottom point. Do not unfold.

3. Pinch the top folded edge and push together. (Look at the next step.)

4. It looks like this. Press flat.

5. Fold the side points (top layer only) to the top point, forming a diamond shape.

6. Fold the side points of the diamond shape to the center.

7. Tuck the top loose points into the little pockets (inside the small triangles) as far as they will go.

8. Carefully unfold the large triangle. Push the back piece out from the inside, to form the bonnet.

9. Carefully bend back the front edge to form the brim.
    Attach ribbons to tie under the child's chin.

1 Fold the bottom edge of the square up to meet the top edge. Crease. Unfold.

Fold the left side over to meet the right side. Crease. Unfold.

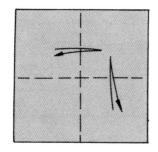

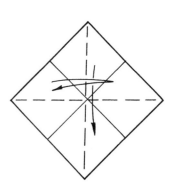

2 Turn over. Put it on the table so it looks like a diamond.

Fold the left point over to meet the right point. Crease. Unfold.

Fold the top point down to meet the bottom point. Do not unfold.

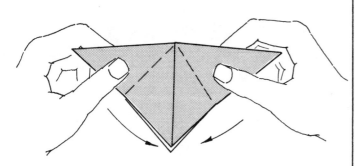

3 Pinch the top folded edge and push together. (Look at the next step.)

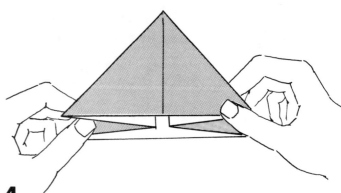

4 It looks like this. Press flat.

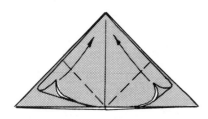

5 Fold the side points (top layer only) to the top point, forming a diamond shape.

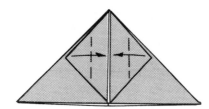

6 Fold the side points of the diamond shape to the center.

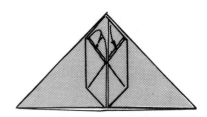

7 Tuck the top loose points into the little pockets (inside the small triangles) as far as they will go.

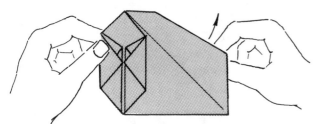

8 Carefully unfold the large triangle. Push the back piece out from the inside, to form the bonnet.

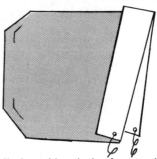

9 Carefully bend back the front edge to form the brim.

Attach ribbons to tie under the child's chin.

Transportation

The Lesson Plan Guide

Objectives

To develop auditory and visual attention skills

To develop temporal-spatial concepts

To develop visual-motor skills

To develop auditory and visual sequencing skills

To teach the concepts and vocabulary that are listed for each model in addition to those listed on page 4

Procedure

Give verbal directions as you demonstrate each step.

Follow-up suggestions

See the Language, Social Studies, Science, and Speech Activities related to the Transportation unit (pp. 92-97).

Have the students close their eyes and revisualize each step of the *Fun Folds* as you recount the steps.

Make an experience chart emphasizing the sequential aspects of the lesson.

Use the *Fun Folds* on the bulletin board or on greeting cards.

Additional suggestions

Additional curriculum-oriented follow-up activities are given for individual *Fun Folds*.

Have the students teach the *Fun Folds* to others. This activity fosters socialization while emphasizing speech and language development.

Language Activities

These activities develop vocabulary, thinking skills, comprehension, and expression of language. Encourage students to reply in a complete sentence. It may be necessary to repeat the students' answers in expanded sentence form until they begin to respond appropriately.

1. Display pictures of various forms of transportation. Guide the students into classifying them in categories:

    Air: plane, helicopter, rocket, hot air balloon, . . .

    Land: car, truck, bus, bicycle, tricycle, wagon, train, . . .

    Sea: boat, water skis, canoe, ocean liner, yacht, schooner, . . .

    Foot power: feet, bicycle, tricycle, . . .

    Blades: ice skates, sled, skis, . . .

    Wheels: bicycle, tricycle, roller skates, skateboard, . . .

    Other: elevator, escalator

2. Use the following vocabulary to describe transportation. Encourage the students to add words to the list and use them in sentences. The students then can draw pictures to illustrate the sentences.

    Adjectives: slow, high, low, bumpy, rough, sleek, shiny, big, fast, sharp, steady, shaky, crisp, . . .

    Irregular past tense verbs:

fly - flew	ride - rode	dive - dove
run - ran	slide - slid	stand - stood

    Irregular plural noun:

    foot - feet

3. Antonyms. Make an "antonym train." Write FIRST on the engine, and LAST on the caboose.

push - pull	fast - slow	on - off
accelerate - brake	mount - dismount	start - stop
leave - arrive	take off - land	deep - shallow
up - down	sail - dock	float - sink

4. Synonyms.

start - begin	leave - depart	up - rise
car - automobile	quick - fast	travel - journey
motor - engine	sail - cruise	arrive - come

5. Homographs. The students can illustrate and write sentences that show the multiple meanings of words (for example, We wear socks on our feet; The bench is three feet long).

plane	blade	fly
train	yard	feet
space	land	pilot

6. Homonyms. Have the students draw pictures or write sentences that show the meanings of homonyms.

plane - plain	hangar - hanger	road - rode - rowed
brake - break	sea - see	fare - fair

7. Similarities and differences. Have the students explain how these transportation words are the same and how they are different:

pilot - engineer	car - bus	bicycle - tricycle
hangar - garage	plane - train	motorcycle - bicycle
elevator - escalator	sled - skis	ice skates - roller skates

8. Categories. This activity develops auditory memory, comprehension, and oral language skills. Have the students repeat each group of words after you. Ask them which word does not belong. Have them explain their choices. (Note: For young students, use picture cards to augment oral presentation.)

roller skates - bicycle - ice skates - wagon	skis - sled - ice skates - tricycle
bicycle - car - tricycle - skateboard	plane - helicopter - rocket - boat
sailboat - helicopter - rowboat - canoe	train - car - bus - truck
bus - car - wagon - truck	

9. Auditory closure. This activity develops vocabulary, thinking skills, verbal expression, and oral language structure. Review the names of people associated with transportation, types of transportation, and where we might expect to see them (air, sea, land). Then have the students listen as you read the sentences. Ask them to supply the missing word. Explain that in each group, we are listening for a person, a place, or a thing.

Who:

A person who flies a plane is a _____ . (pilot)

A person who sails a boat is a _____ . (sailor, captain)

A person who drives a bus is a _____ . (driver)

A person who runs a train is an _____ . (engineer)

A person who rides on a train, plane, bus is a _____ . (passenger)

A person who flies a spaceship is an _____ . (astronaut)

A person who walks is a _____ . (pedestrian)

Where:

A plane flies in the _____ . (sky)

A train runs on _____ . (tracks)

A horse gallops on a _____ . (path)

A bus travels on the _____ . (road)

A boat sails on the _____ . (water)

A spaceship flies into _____ . (space)

We ice skate at a _____ . (rink)

What:

A sail is part of a _____ . (sailboat)

A blade is part of a _____ . (helicopter, skate)

A wing is part of a _____ . (plane)

A hoof is part of a _____ . (horse)

A caboose is part of a _____ . (train)

A steering wheel is part of a _____ . (bus, car, truck)

A booster is part of a _____ . (rocket ship)

10. Crossword puzzle and word scramble. This activity develops visual sequencing, visual memory, and visual motor skills. Reproduce and distribute the following worksheet.

Answer key: DOWN—skate, helicopter, sail, canoe, train, feet

ACROSS—hop, fly, truck, pony, boat, cart, raft, plane, horse, taxi

"Transportation" Worksheet

Name _____ Date _____

Directions: Unscramble the "Transportation" words.
Then, using the letter clues, fill in the Rocket Ship Crossword Puzzle.

DOWN	ACROSS
atske	poh
clheioptre	ylf
asil	rkuct
coena	pyno
riatn	bato
efet	rtca
	traf
	lpnea
	oersh
	axti

Social Studies Activities

1. Display a map of your city, a United States map, and a world map or a globe. Discuss different forms of transportation. How do you travel:

   From one classroom to another?

   From home to school?

   From a particular state to another?

   From a particular country to another?

2. Compare forms of transportation used in the past. Discuss the Indians' use of canoes, and the forms of transportation used by Columbus and by the Pilgrims. (See the "Life on the Water" unit for appropriate *Fun Folds* to accompany the discussion.)

3. Discuss modern (present-day) forms of transportation. Discuss how transportation has changed our way of life.

4. Prepare a timeline showing the progress of transportation.

5. Visit an airport, bus terminal, or train station. Teach the vocabulary words *passenger, ticket, fare.*

Science Activities

1. Compare different forms of transportation by how fast they can go. Prepare a chart to show the slowest to fastest forms of transportation.

2. Have the students make *Fun Folds* airplanes and hold races.

3. Use *Fun Folds* airplanes to measure distance and gliding time. You will need a stopwatch, markers, paper and pencil, and a tape measure. Have the students fly their planes indoors. Chart the flying and gliding time of each plane on a bar graph. Then have them fly their planes outdoors. Note the difference in distance and gliding time when wind is a factor.

Sample bar graphs:

Indoors

plane C
plane B
plane A
_____
Distance (yards)

plane C
plane B
plane A
_____
Gliding time

Outdoors

plane C
plane B
plane A
_____
Distance (yards)

plane C
plane B
plane A
_____
Gliding time

Speech Activities

The following are excellent as carryover activities for articulation therapy, voice therapy, and fluency practice.

1. Have the students teach "Transportation" *Fun Folds* to others. This activity provides an opportunity for students to practice tension-free vocal quality and improve pitch, volume, and rate. Children who stutter can build confidence as they practice fluent speech.

2. Make *Fun Folds* and practice appropriate tongue twisters (for example, a *Fun Folds* sled: "Slide the sled across a smooth surface").

3. Make (or purchase) a target with scoring points. Divide it into quarters. In each section, write a word containing the students' speech sounds. Have the students make airplane *Fun Folds* to shoot at the target. Points are awarded for each word hit and correctly articulated.

4. Make a "good speech train." On the cars, write words or mount pictures (or Peel & Put® stickers) of objects containing the students' speech sounds. As the students articulate the words correctly, they move from the caboose to the engine.

Sailboat (Single Sail)

This model is suitable for very young children.

To further simplify this model, use a triangle (made from a square cut on the diagonal) and begin with Step 4.

Concepts and vocabulary (*See also* page 4)

rotate

decorate

sail

boat

Materials

A square of thin paper

Crayons or marking pens (optional)

Additional suggestions

Make this model in three sizes. Teach the concept of small, smaller, and smallest.

Place boats on a sheet of construction paper. Discuss and teach distance words:
near and far
near, nearer, nearest
far, farther, farthest

How to fold the Sailboat

1. Put a square of paper on the table.

2. Turn it so it looks like a diamond.

3. Fold the bottom point up to meet the top point. Now you have a triangle.

4. Fold the left point over to meet the right point. Crease. Unfold.

5. Bring the right side of the triangle over to meet the center crease. Press flat.

6. Rotate the model so the larger triangle is pointing up.

7. Fold the bottom point behind, to make a flat edge.

8. Decorate the sail.

1 Put a square of paper on the table.

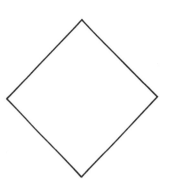

2 Turn it so it looks like a diamond.

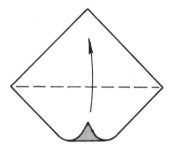

3 Fold the bottom point up to meet the top point. Now you have a triangle.

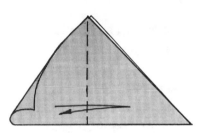

4 Fold the left point over to meet the right point. Crease. Unfold.

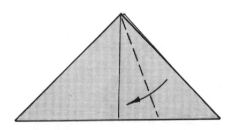

5 Bring the right side of the triangle over to meet the center crease. Press flat.

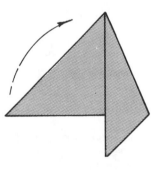

6 Rotate the model so the larger triangle is pointing up.

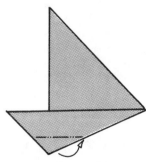

7 Fold the bottom point behind, to make a flat edge.

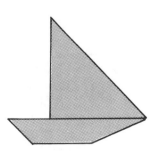

8 Decorate the sail.

Rowboat

This model lends itself to other creations. If you stop at Step 6, you have a note holder, suitable for a child's bulletin board. If you use red or pink paper, stop after Step 7, turn it over, and you will have made a kiss (lips). See what other creations can be made from this general form. Usually, children can invent some of their own.

Concepts and vocabulary (*See also* page 4)

both

only

last

rowboat

Materials

A 6-inch or larger square of thin paper that is colored on one side

An additional suggestion

Discuss other types of boats. See "Life on the Water" for additional *Fun Folds* boats.

How to fold the Rowboat

1. Place a square of paper on the table so the colored side is facing you. Fold the bottom edge to the top.

2. Fold the bottom folded edge to the top again. Press flat. Open the last fold you made.

3. Using the top layer only, fold the top left corner down to the center crease to form a triangle. Repeat with the other corner.

4. Bring the lower corners (both layers) up to the center crease.

5. Fold the top layer only down to the bottom. Turn over.

6. Now it looks like this.

7. Fold the upper corners down to the center crease to form triangles.

8. Fold the top down to the bottom.

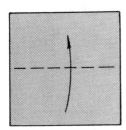

1 Place a square of paper on the table so the colored side is facing you. Fold the bottom edge to the top.

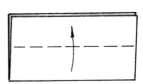

2 Fold the bottom folded edge to the top again. Press flat. Open the last fold you made.

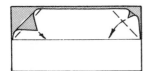

3 Using the top layer only, fold the top left corner down to the center crease to form a triangle. Repeat with the other corner.

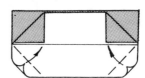

4 Bring the lower corners (both layers) up to the center crease.

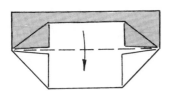

5 Fold the top layer only down to the bottom. Turn over.

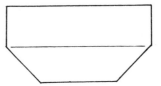

6 Now it looks like this.

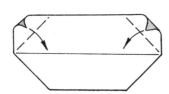

7 Fold the upper corners down to the center crease to form triangles.

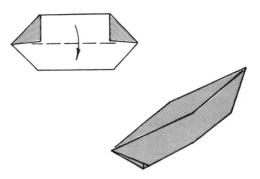

8 Fold the top down to the bottom.

Helicopter

This wonderful action model does not rely on accuracy in folding or cutting.

Hint

You may wish to reproduce a pattern with cut lines and dots drawn in.

Concepts and vocabulary (*See also* page 4)

half

drop

allows

almost

twirl

helicopter

Materials

A 2-inch by 8-inch rectangle of paper

Scissors

Additional suggestions

Discuss various uses for helicopters.

Name other things that fly.

How to fold the Helicopter

1. Put a rectangle of paper on the table with the short sides at the top and bottom. Cut along the center of the rectangle, almost down to the midpoint, as shown.

2. At the center, make two small cuts, as shown.

3. Fold the lower left edge over to the right, as far as the cut allows.

4. Repeat with the lower right edge.

5. Fold the lower left corner over to form a triangle, as shown.

6. Fold the upper left piece backward as far as the cut allows.
    Fold the upper right piece forward as far as the cut allows.

7. Hold it high and drop it. Watch it twirl its way to the floor.

1 Put a rectangle of paper on the table with the short sides at the top and bottom. Cut along the center of the rectangle, almost down to the midpoint, as shown.

2 At the center, make two small cuts, as shown.

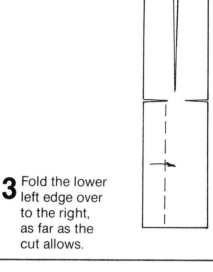

3 Fold the lower left edge over to the right, as far as the cut allows.

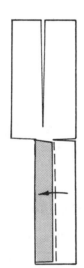

4 Repeat with the lower right edge.

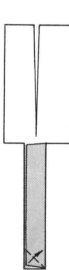

5 Fold the lower left corner over to form a triangle, as shown.

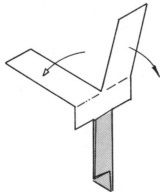

6 Fold the upper left piece backward as far as the cut allows.

Fold the upper right piece forward as far as the cut allows.

7 Hold it high and drop it. Watch it twirl its way to the floor.

Airplane

Hints

This model requires symmetry to fly well. Be sure that each side of every step is folded evenly. Have the children practice making this fold with thin paper before they progress to heavier stock.

Concepts and vocabulary (*See also* page 4)

peak

base

toss

roof

flap

airplane

Materials

An 8½-inch by 11-inch rectangle of stiff paper

Additional suggestions

Have an airplane-flying contest.

Discuss things that fly.

How to fold the Airplane

1. Place a rectangle of paper on the table with the shorter sides on the top and bottom. Fold the left side over to meet the right side. It looks like a book.

2. Unfold.

3. Fold the left corner down to the dot, as shown. Repeat with the right corner.

4. Now it looks like a house. Fold the "peak of the roof" down to the "base of the roof."

5. Fold the top corners down to the dot, as shown.

6. Now it looks like this.

7. Fold the left side over to meet the right side.

8. Fold the top flap over to the left along the dotted line.

9. Turn over. Fold the top flap over to the right along the dotted line.

10. Toss it in the air!

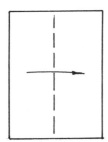

1 Place a rectangle of paper on the table with the shorter sides on the top and bottom. Fold the left side over to meet the right side. It looks like a book.

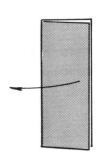

2 Unfold.

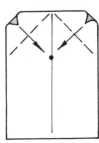

3 Fold the left corner down to the dot, as shown. Repeat with the right corner.

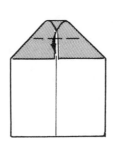

4 Now it looks like a house. Fold the "peak of the roof" down to the "base of the roof."

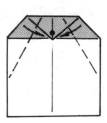

5 Fold the top corners down to the dot, as shown.

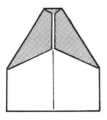

6 Now it looks like this.

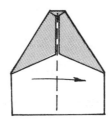

7 Fold the left side over to meet the right side.

8 Fold the top flap over to the left along the dotted line.

9 Turn over. Fold the top flap over to the right along the dotted line.

10 Toss it in the air!

Horse

Hint

Note that Steps 7 and 8 are almost the same. In the latter, the fold is made closer to the open end.

Concepts and vocabulary (*See also* page 4)

aside

together

hooves

legs

mane

horse

Materials

An 8½-inch by 11-inch or 9-inch by 12-inch rectangle of paper, cut in half lengthwise

A stapler

Scissors and paper scraps for mane and tail

Additional suggestions

Fold the Wagon to go with the Horse.

Discuss other animals that are used for transportation.

How to fold the Horse

1. Put one rectangle of paper on the table with the long edges at the top and bottom. Fold the bottom edge up to meet the top edge. Crease. Unfold.

2. Fold the top edge down to the center crease. Fold the bottom edge up to the center crease.

3. Fold in half by bringing the top folded edge down to meet the bottom folded edge.

4. Repeat Steps 1 through 3 with the other rectangle. Now you have two strips.

5. Fold each strip of folded paper in half, bringing the right short sides over to meet the left short sides.

6. Set one piece aside.

7. Fold the top flap down, as shown.
   Turn over and repeat on the back.
   This makes the head and front legs of the horse.

8. Now, using the piece you set aside, fold the top flap down, as shown.
   Turn over. Repeat on the back.
   This makes the body and back legs of the horse.

9. Put the back leg piece between the front head piece.

10. Staple them together, as shown. Add a mane and tail.

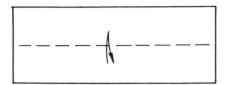

1 Put one rectangle of paper on the table with the long edges at the top and bottom. Fold the bottom edge up to meet the top edge. Crease. Unfold.

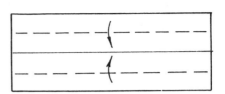

2 Fold the top edge down to the center crease. Fold the bottom edge up to the center crease.

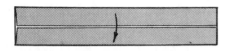

3 Fold in half by bringing the top folded edge down to meet the bottom folded edge.

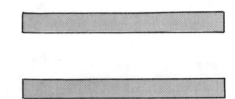

4 Repeat Steps 1 through 3 with the other rectangle. Now you have two strips.

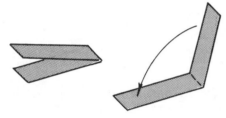

5 Fold each strip of folded paper in half, bringing the right short sides over to meet the left short sides.

6 Set one piece aside.

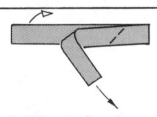

7 Fold the top flap down, as shown.

Turn over and repeat on the back.

This makes the head and front legs of the horse.

8 Now, using the piece you set aside, fold the top flap down, as shown.

Turn over. Repeat on the back.

This makes the body and back legs of the horse.

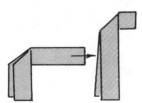

9 Put the back leg piece between the front head piece.

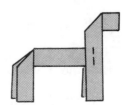

10 Staple them together, as shown. Add a mane and tail.

Wagon Base

This is not a suitable model for very young children, because it requires accuracy in folding.

Hint

In Step 7, be sure you are folding right triangles. These triangles should *not* reach the center crease.

Concepts and vocabulary (*See also* page 4)

each	careful
complete	base
stand	straight
pockets	

Materials

Use an 8½-inch by 11-inch rectangle of thin paper.

After the children have made the Wagon Base with thin paper, have them make a sturdier model with construction paper.

Additional suggestions (See page 111)

Make the cover and wheels for the Wagon. (See pattern on page 110.)

Make the Horse to go with the completed Wagon.

Add a handle, and use the Wagon Base as an Easter Basket.

Make another Wagon Base from a rectangle cut about ¼-inch narrower and shorter. Use it for the bottom of a Gift Box. Use the Wagon Base, above, for the top of the Gift Box.

How to fold the Wagon Base

1. Put a rectangle of paper on the table with the short edges on the top and bottom. Fold the bottom edge up to the top. Crease. Unfold.

2. Fold the top edge down to the center crease. Fold the bottom edge up to the center crease.

3. Fold the left side over to meet the right side.

4. It looks like a book. Crease. Unfold.

5. Fold the left side to the center crease. Repeat with the right side. Crease well.

6. Open the left and right sides.

7. Fold each outside corner in to the dots, as shown. Be careful! Look at Step 8.

8. Fold the upper layer of paper up over the triangular flaps as far as it will go. Repeat to cover the lower triangles.

9. Put your thumbs inside the "pockets" and gently pull apart.

10. Pinch each corner to make the sides stand straight.

Turn to page 110 for the pattern to make a cover and wheels for the wagon.

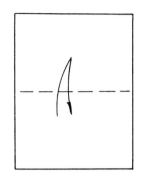

1 Put a rectangle of paper on the table with the short edges on the top and bottom. Fold the bottom edge up to the top. Crease. Unfold.

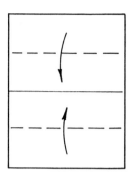

2 Fold the top edge down to the center crease. Fold the bottom edge up to the center crease.

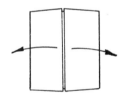

3 Fold the left side over to meet the right side.

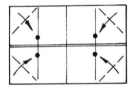

4 It looks like a book. Crease. Unfold.

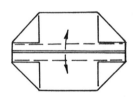

5 Fold the left side to the center crease. Repeat with the right side. Crease well.

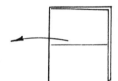

6 Open the left and right sides.

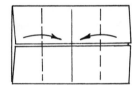

7 Fold each outside corner in to the dots, as shown. Be careful! Look at Step 8.

8 Fold the upper layer of paper up over the triangular flaps as far as it will go. Repeat to cover the lower triangles.

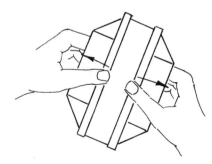

9 Put your thumbs inside the "pockets" and gently pull apart.

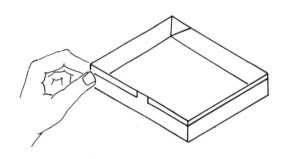

10 Pinch each corner to make the sides stand straight.

Cover and Wheel Patterns

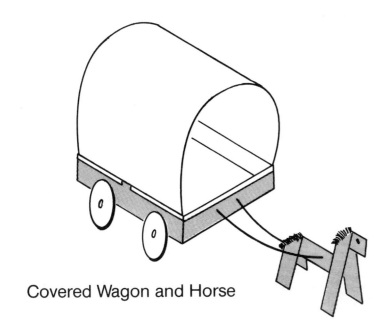

Covered Wagon and Horse

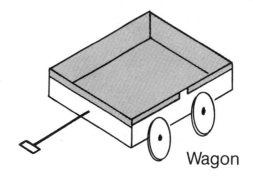

Wagon

Gift Box

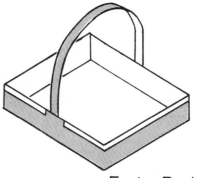

Easter Basket

Sled

When Step 4 is completed, it looks like a house. Have the children "huff and puff and blow the house down."

Concepts and vocabulary (*See also* page 4)

itself

again

complete

sharp

dull

runners

Materials

A 6-inch or larger square of thin paper

An additional suggestion

Discuss equipment used for winter sports.

How to fold the Sled

1. Put a square of paper on the table. Fold the left side over to meet the right side.

2. Unfold.

3. Fold the left top corner down to the dot, as shown.

4. Repeat with the right top corner, as shown.

5. It looks like a house.
   Now fold the left side of the house to the center crease to begin making the runners.

6. Unfold the crease you just made.

(continued on page 114)

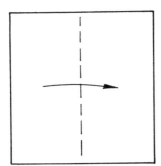

1 Put a square of paper on the table. Fold the left side over to meet the right side.

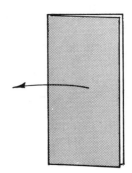

2 Unfold.

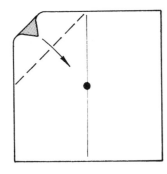

3 Fold the left top corner down to the dot, as shown.

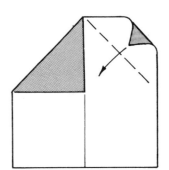

4 Repeat with the right top corner, as shown.

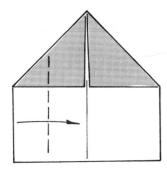

5 It looks like a house.
Now fold the left side of the house to the center crease to begin making the runners.

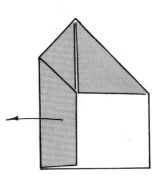

6 Unfold the crease you just made.

How to fold the Sled (continued)

7. Fold the left side to the crease you made in Step 5.

8. Fold the left folded side over onto itself.

9. Fold the left side over on itself again, so it meets the center crease. This completes one of the runners.

10. Repeat Steps 5 through 9 with the right side to complete the other runner.

11. Turn over. Stand the sled up on its runners and slide it across a smooth surface.

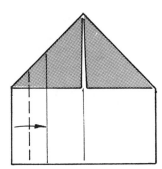

7 Fold the left side to the crease you made in Step 5.

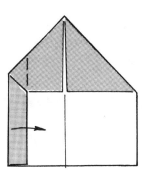

8 Fold the left folded side over onto itself.

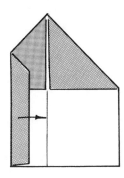

9 Fold the left side over on itself again, so it meets the center crease. This completes one of the runners.

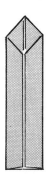

10 Repeat Steps 5 through 9 with the right side to complete the other runner.

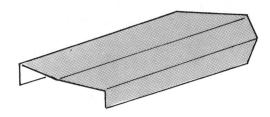

11 Turn over. Stand the sled up on its runners and slide it across a smooth surface.

Rocket Ship

Hints

This model is rather difficult. Be sure that Steps 1 through 4 are folded carefully.

Step 6 shows a triangle with two flaps on each side. Many advanced models begin with this triangular base.

Concepts and vocabulary (*See also* page 4)

finished

base

shown

flaps

rocket ship

first

second

last

another

newly formed

complete

part

Materials

Two 8-inch squares of thin paper

Additional suggestions

Encourage the students to experiment with the completed parts. More stages can be added to the Rocket Ship.

Use this model to teach the concepts of halves, quarters, and eighths.

How to fold the Rocket Ship

1. Put one square of paper on the table. Fold the bottom edge up to meet the top edge. Crease. Unfold.

2. Fold the left side over to meet the right side. Crease. Unfold.

3. Turn over. Put it down so it looks like a diamond. Fold the left point over to meet the right point. Crease. Unfold.

4. Fold the top point down to the bottom point.

5. Pinch the triangle between your fingers and push downward toward the middle.

6. It looks like this.

(continued on page 118)

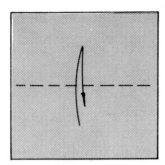

1 Put one square of paper on the table. Fold the bottom edge up to meet the top edge. Crease. Unfold.

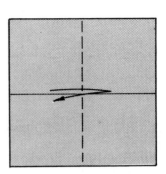

2 Fold the left side over to meet the right side. Crease. Unfold.

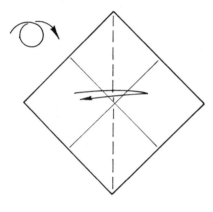

3 Turn over. Put it down so it looks like a diamond. Fold the left point over to meet the right point. Crease. Unfold.

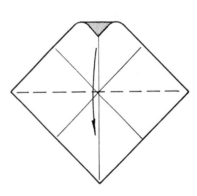

4 Fold the top point down to the bottom point.

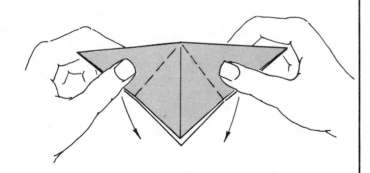

5 Pinch the triangle between your fingers and push downward toward the middle.

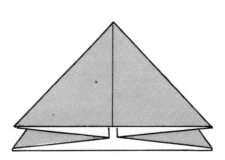

6 It looks like this.

How to fold the Rocket Ship (continued)

7. Using the top flaps only, bring the folded edges downward to meet the center crease.

8. Turn over. Repeat on the back.

9. One part of the rocket is now complete. It looks like this.
   Now go back to Step 1 and make another one, using the other square of paper.

10. Open the last fold on each flap, on the one you just made.

11. Fold the outer folded edges down to the newly formed creases, as shown. Repeat on the other three flaps.

12. Push the lower points of the first part between the layers of the second part.

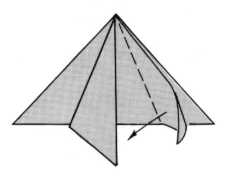

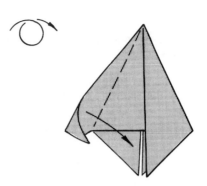

7 Using the top flaps only, bring the folded edges downward to meet the center crease.

8 Turn over. Repeat on the back.

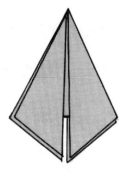

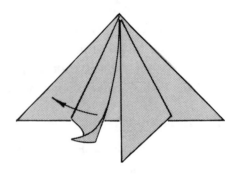

9 One part of the rocket is now complete. It looks like this.

Now go back to Step 1 and make another one, using the other square of paper.

10 Open the last fold on each flap, on the one you just made.

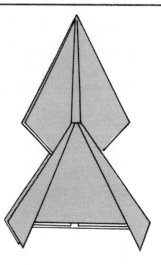

11 Fold the outer folded edges down to the newly formed creases, as shown. Repeat on the other three flaps.

12 Push the lower points of the first part between the layers of the second part.

Boot

Hint

At Step 11, the distance between the lines is critical to the final shape of the boot. It should be about 1/16-inch wider than the boot's top band.

Concepts and vocabulary (*See also* page 4)

overlap

same

flap

whole

index finger

band

blade

Materials

A 6-inch square of thin paper

Additional suggestions

At Christmas time, make the Boot as a Christmas stocking ornament. Use paper that is colored on one side. Begin with the white side facing you, to make a boot with a white band at the top.

For St. Patrick's Day, use green paper to make a Leprechaun's Boot. Turn the toes upward.

Use the instructions on page 124 to make roller skates or ice skates.

How to fold the Boot

1. Put a square of paper on the table so it looks like a diamond.
   Fold the left point over to meet the right point. Crease. Unfold.

2. Fold the lower left and right sides up to meet the center crease.

3. It looks like an ice-cream cone. Turn over.

4. Fold the top point down as far as it will go.

5. Unfold the triangle you just made.

6. Fold the top point down to the crease.

7. Fold the folded edge down to the same crease.

8. Fold the whole top piece over the cone. Crease.

9. Fold the bottom point up to the top edge.

(continued on page 122)

1 Put a square of paper on the table so it looks like a diamond.
Fold the left point over to meet the right point. Crease. Unfold.

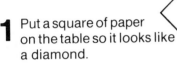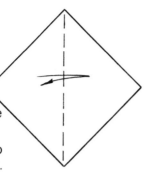

2 Fold the lower left and right sides up to meet the center crease.

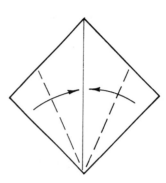

3 It looks like an ice-cream cone. Turn over.

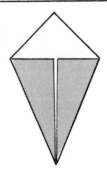

4 Fold the top point down as far as it will go.

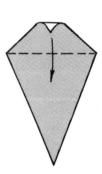

5 Unfold the triangle you just made.

6 Fold the top point down to the crease.

7 Fold the folded edge down to the same crease.

8 Fold the whole top piece over the cone. Crease.

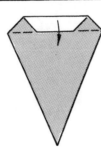

9 Fold the bottom point up to the top edge.

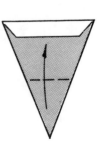

How to fold the Boot (continued)

10. Put your index finger along the lower edge. Fold the top flap down over your finger.

11. Press it flat.

12. Fold the left and right sides away from you as you fold the model in half.

13. Pick up the model and pinch, as shown. Pull the toe over to one side. Press it flat.

14. Now unfold the top layer.

15. Bend the left and right sides in to overlap. Tuck the right band into the left band.

16. This is how it looks from the back.

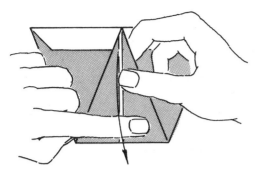

10 Put your index finger along the lower edge. Fold the top flap down over your finger.

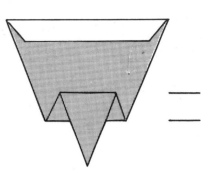

11 Press it flat.

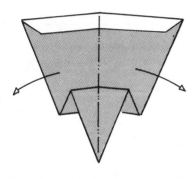

12 Fold the left and right sides away from you as you fold the model in half.

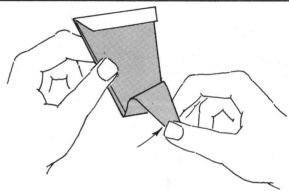

13 Pick up the model and pinch, as shown. Pull the toe over to one side. Press it flat.

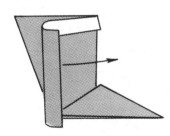

14 Now unfold the top layer.

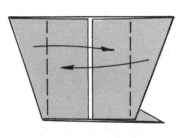

15 Bend the left and right sides in to overlap. Tuck the right band into the left band.

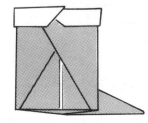

16 This is how it looks from the back.

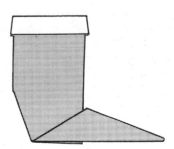

Skate Patterns

These patterns will fit a boot made from a 6-inch
square of paper.

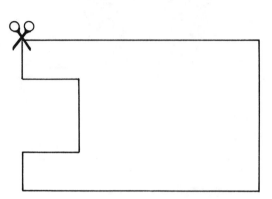

1 Cut out this shape.

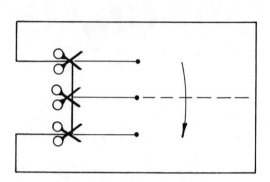

2 Make three parallel cuts to the dots.
Fold the top edge down to meet the bottom edge.

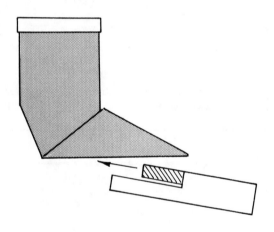

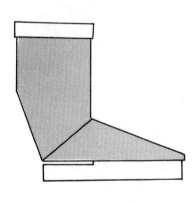

3 Slide the shaded part into the pockets under the boot to make an ice skate.

OR—

Glue cereal rounds or small circles of stiff paper
under the boot to make a roller skate.

Life on the Water

The Lesson Plan Guide

Objectives

To develop auditory and visual attention skills

To develop temporal-spatial concepts

To develop visual-motor skills

To develop auditory and visual sequencing skills

To teach the concepts and vocabulary that are listed for each model in addition to those listed on page 4

Procedure

Give verbal directions as you demonstrate each step.

Follow-up suggestions

See the Language, Social Studies, Science, and Speech Activities related to Life on the Water (pp. 128-133).

Have the students close their eyes and revisualize each step of the *Fun Folds* as you recount the steps.

Make an experience chart emphasizing the sequential aspects of the lesson.

Use the *Fun Folds* on the bulletin board or on greeting cards.

Additional suggestions

Additional curriculum-oriented activities are given for individual *Fun Folds*.

Have the students teach the *Fun Folds* to others. This activity fosters socialization while emphasizing speech and language development.

Language Activities

These activities develop vocabulary, thinking skills, comprehension, and expression of language. Encourage students to reply in a complete sentence. It may be necessary to repeat the students' answers in expanded sentence form until they begin to respond appropriately.

1. Display pictures of bodies of water, sailing vessels, animals that live in water, waterfowl, and fishing equipment. Label, discuss, and classify the pictures as shown below.

   ocean, pond, lake, river, stream, brook, swamp, . . .
   sailboat, rowboat, canoe, ocean liner, motorboat, yacht, schooner, . . .
   whale, alligator, crab, octopus, shark, frog, fish, . . .
   swan, seagull, duck, pelican, . . .
   net, hook, fishing rod, reel, line, . . .

2. Use the following vocabulary to describe "Life on the Water." Encourage the students to add words to the list and use them in sentences. The students then can draw pictures to illustrate the sentences.

   Adjectives: huge, gigantic, puny, little, deep, shallow, high, low, fast, quick, speedy, shiny, breezy, salty, rough, smooth, swift, rapid, few, many, . . .

   Irregular past tense verbs:

swim - swam	sink - sank	wet - wet
catch - caught	blow - blew	ride - rode
fly - flew		

   Irregular plural nouns:

   fly - flies
   fish - fish (when referring to the same class of fish)

3. Antonyms. Play "Antonym Alligators!" Write antonym word pairs on *Fun Folds* alligators.

float - sink	deep - shallow	fast - slow
land - sea	wet - dry	rough - smooth

4. Synonyms. Play "Synonym Sailboats!" Write synonyms on *Fun Folds* sailboats.

low - shallow	quick - fast	huge - gigantic
speedy - rapid	little - small	motor - engine

5. Homographs. The students can illustrate and write sentences that show the multiple meanings of words (for example, Let's wave to mother; The big wave knocked me over).

scale	fish	sink
line	duck	water
deck		

6. Homonyms. Have the students draw pictures or write sentences that show the meanings of homonyms.

tail - tale	whale - wail	bale - bail
sail - sale	sole - soul	oar - ore - or
tide - tied	pail - pale	rowed - road - rode
reel - real	sea - see	

7. Similarities and differences. Have the students explain how these words go together and how they are different.

rowboat - sailboat	mouth - beak	paddle - oar
canoe - motorboat	aquarium - zoo	ocean - pond
wing - fin	turtle - crab	yacht - ocean liner

8. Categories. This activity develops auditory memory, comprehension, and oral language skills. Have the students repeat each group of words after you. Ask them which word does not belong. Have them explain their choices. (Note: For young students, use picture cards to augment oral presentation.)

> rod - reel - hook - bail
> shark - whale - seagull - octopus
> alligator - pelican - turtle - fish
> ship - sailboat - rowboat - bus
> pond - stream - field - brook

9. Comparatives. Make three *Fun Folds* ships of different sizes. Teach the concept of big, bigger, biggest.

10. Rhyming story. This activity develops auditory discrimination, auditory closure, auditory memory, auditory sequencing, auditory comprehension, and oral language skills. Read the story aloud, emphasizing the underlined rhyming words. (For a visual closure activity, provide a copy of the story, page 130.)

Life on the Water

> Melissa and Michael were reading a book
> While sitting alongside a babbling <u>brook</u>.
> They saw two big bullfrogs jump close to a boat
> While playing at leapfrog and trying to <u>float</u>.
> A pelican, seen with a fish in its beak,
> Was sad to discover its beak was too <u>weak,</u>
> So back in the water it dropped that big fish
> Instead of enjoying a freshly caught <u>dish</u>.
> Melissa and Michael then saw an old shoe
> That drifted up next to a leaky <u>canoe</u>.
> To their great surprise, just a little while later,
> That shoe was gulped down by a big <u>alligator</u>!

11. Matching relationships. This activity can be presented in oral and written form.

> A beak belongs to a _____ . (bird)
> A fin belongs to a _____ . (fish)
> A shell belongs to a _____ . (turtle, snail, crab)
> A wave belongs to the _____ . (ocean, lake)
> A sail belongs to a _____ . (sailboat)
> A wing belongs to a _____ . (bird)
> A paddle belongs to a _____ . (canoe)
> An oar belongs to a _____ . (rowboat)

12. Crossword puzzle and word scramble. This activity develops visual sequencing, visual memory, and visual-motor skills. Reproduce and distribute the worksheet on page 131.

   Answer key: DOWN—swan, sailboat, fish, reel

   ACROSS—whale, fin, scale, hook

"Life on the Water" Worksheet

Name _____ Date _____

Melissa and Michael were reading a book

While sitting alongside a babbling_____ .

They saw two big bullfrogs jump close to a boat

While playing at leapfrog and trying to _____ .

A pelican, seen with a fish in its beak,

Was sad to discover its beak was too _____ ,

So back in the water it dropped that big fish

Instead of enjoying a freshly caught _____ .

Melissa and Michael then saw an old shoe

That drifted up next to a leaky _____ .

To their great surprise, just a little while later,

That shoe was gulped down by a big _____ !

"Life on the Water" Worksheet

Name _____ Date _____

Directions: Unscramble the "Life on the Water" words.
Then, using the letter clues, fill in the Sailboat Crossword Puzzle.

DOWN

wasn

laisaobt

hifs

eler

ACROSS

leawh

inf

leacs

koho

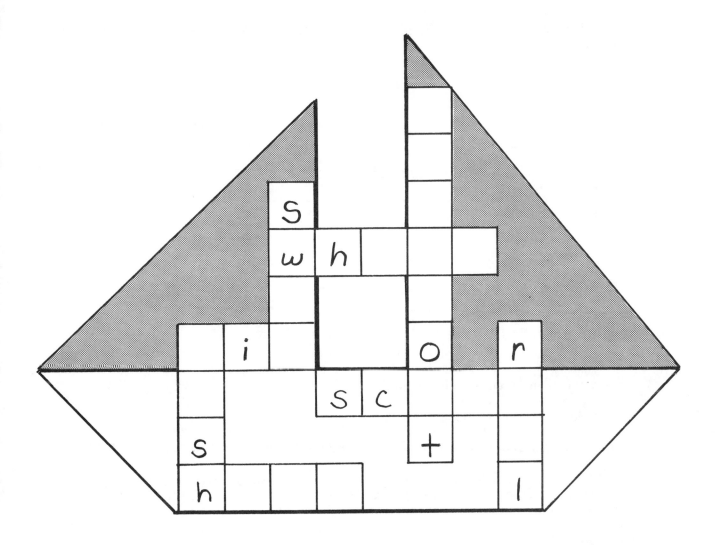

Social Studies Activities

Vikings: Make a *Fun Folds* Viking hat. Discuss sailors of long ago.

Columbus Day: Make three *Fun Folds* boats representing the *Nina,* the *Pinta,* and the *Santa Maria.* Teach the vocabulary words *discover* and *voyage.* Discuss Columbus' voyage to America. Discuss life on the boats during the journey to America.

Indian Life: Make a *Fun Folds* canoe. Discuss how the Indians used the canoe as a form of transportation.

Thanksgiving: Discuss the Pilgrims' means of transportation to the New World. Make a *Fun Folds* sailboat to represent the *Mayflower.*

Prepare a Thanksgiving feast. Send *Fun Folds* invitations to the feast. Use *Fun Folds* sailboats as place cards.

Prepare a chart to show the life of the Pilgrims in the New World. Compare their lives to ours.

Sample chart:

	Pilgrims	Our Lives Today
Environment		
Homes		
Clothing		
Hunting methods		
Food supplies		
Transportation		

Science Activities

1. Visit an aquarium. Discuss the fish seen there.

2. Discuss various types of fish that live together.

3. Prepare a bulletin board "aquarium" in the classroom. Mount "Life on the Water" *Fun Folds.*

4. Visit the seashore and collect seashells (or ask a student who has been to the ocean to bring seashells to the classroom). Discuss and classify the shells. Prepare a display of seashells, and invite other students to view the collection.

5. Have the students prepare reports on bodies of water, sea life, and so on.

6. Have the students write essays on endangered mammals (for example, the whale) and hold a panel discussion on the topic.

Speech Activities

The following are excellent as carryover activities for articulation therapy, voice therapy, and fluency practice.

1. Have the students teach "Life on the Water" *Fun Folds* to others. This activity provides an opportunity for students to practice tension-free vocal quality and improve pitch, volume, and rate. Children who stutter can build confidence as they practice fluent speech.

2. Have students blow *Fun Folds* sailboats across their desks to teach sustained air flow.

3. Play "Articulation Fishing." Make *Fun Folds* goldfish. On the fish, write words or mount pictures (or *Peel & Put*® stickers) of objects containing the target sound. Attach a paper clip to each fish. Make a fishing pole from a stick, string, and a small magnet. When the students "catch a fish," they say "Sam the Sailor went fishing for a _____." If the sound is misarticulated, the fish is thrown back "in the water." The student who has the most fish wins the game.

Basic Sailboat

This boat has no complicated folds and is ideal for young children.
Very young children can begin with a triangle at Step 4.

Concepts and vocabulary (*See also* page 4)

    sailboat

    lift

Materials

    A 6-inch or larger square of thin paper

An additional suggestion

    Make three boats of varying sizes. Teach the concept of big, bigger, biggest.

How to fold the Basic Sailboat

1. Put a square of paper on the table.

2. Turn the square so it looks like a diamond.

3. Lift the bottom point up to meet the top point. Press it flat.

4. Now you have a triangle.

5. Lift the bottom edge up a little bit. Press it flat.

1 Put a square of paper on the table.

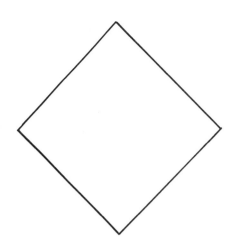

2 Turn the square so it looks like a diamond.

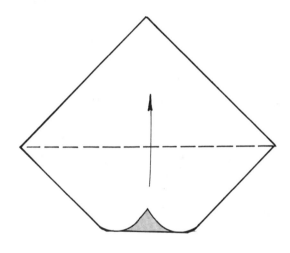

3 Lift the bottom point up to meet the top point. Press it flat.

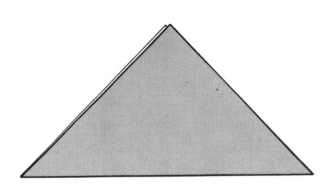

4 Now you have a triangle.

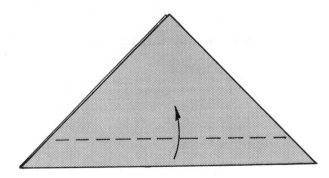

5 Lift the bottom edge up a little bit. Press it flat.

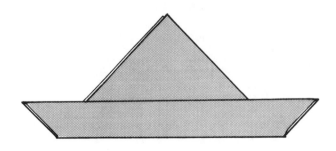

Sailor with Hat

This fold is suitable for younger children.

Hint

In Step 5, be sure to fold each layer up as far as the paper allows.

Concepts and vocabulary (*See also* page 4)

set aside

piece

sailor

allow

half

Materials

An 8½-inch by 11-inch rectangle of thin paper

Scissors

Pencil or marking pens or crayons

Additional suggestions

Make two sailors and hats. Give one a happy face, the other a sad face. Discuss emotions. Discuss different types of head coverings (football helmet, nurse's cap, and so on).

How to fold the Sailor with Hat

1. Put a rectangle of paper on the table with the long edges at the top and bottom. Fold the left (short) side over to meet the right side. Unfold. Cut in half.

2. Put the short sides of each rectangle on the top and bottom. Fold the top of each piece down. Set aside one piece, to use later for the sailor's face.

3. The hat: On the other piece of paper, fold the left side over to meet the right side. Crease. Open that fold.

4. Fold the right and left top corners down to the dots, as shown. Make sure the open edge is at the bottom.

5. There are two layers at the bottom. Fold up one layer as far as the triangles allow. Turn over and repeat on the back layer.

6. The face: Use the other piece of paper. Fold in the four corners a little bit, making triangles.

7. Turn over. Draw a face.

8. Tuck the face into the hat.

1 Put a rectangle of paper on the table with the long edges at the top and bottom.
Fold the left (short) side over to meet the right side. Unfold. Cut in half.

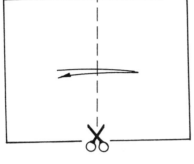

2 Put the short sides of each rectangle on the top and bottom. Fold the top of each piece down. Set aside one piece, to use later for the sailor's face.

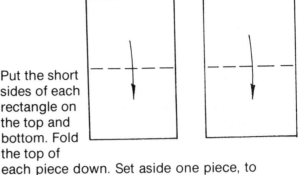

3 The hat: On the other piece of paper, fold the left side over to meet the right side. Crease. Open that fold.

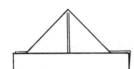

4 Fold the right and left top corners down to the dots, as shown. Make sure the open edge is at the bottom.

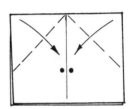

5 There are two layers at the bottom. Fold up one layer as far as the triangles allow. Turn over and repeat on the back layer.

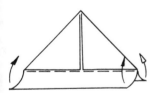

6 The face: Use the other piece of paper. Fold in the four corners a little bit, making triangles.

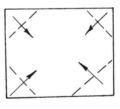

7 Turn over. Draw a face.

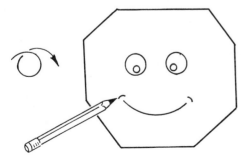

8 Tuck the face into the hat.

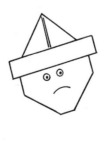

Sailboat (Double Sails)

This model is suitable for very young children.

Hint

Step 2 is the only tricky step. Make sure that every bit of the right and left triangles is folded up.

Concepts and vocabulary (*See also* page 4)

halfway

straight

discover

cover

turn around

sailboat

most

Materials

A triangle of thin paper (made from a square cut on the diagonal), colored on one side

Additional suggestions

Use this model as stand-up place cards, on greeting cards, and on seasonal bulletin boards.
For Columbus Day, make three boats representing the *Nina, Pinta,* and *Santa Maria.*
Use at Thanksgiving as the *Mayflower.*

How to fold the Sailboat

1. Begin with the white side up. Put the triangle on the table with the longest side toward you. Fold the top point straight down so it just meets the bottom edge of the triangle.

2. You now have three triangles. Fold Triangle 1 up along the dotted line. Now it covers part of the center triangle. Repeat with Triangle 3.

3. Now the two side triangles cover most of the center triangle.

4. Fold the bottom point halfway up to form a small triangle.

5. Pull the small triangle forward (toward you) to make a stand.

6. Turn it around to discover a sailboat!

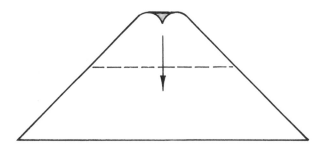

1 Begin with the white side up. Put the triangle on the table with the longest side toward you. Fold the top point straight down so it just meets the bottom edge of the triangle.

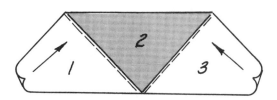

2 You now have three triangles. Fold Triangle 1 up along the dotted line. Now it covers part of the center triangle. Repeat with Triangle 3.

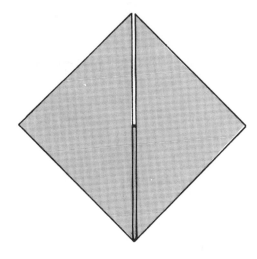

3 Now the two side triangles cover most of the center triangle.

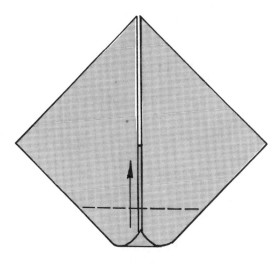

4 Fold the bottom point halfway up to form a small triangle.

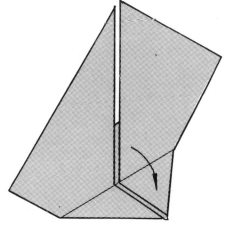

5 Pull the small triangle forward (toward you) to make a stand.

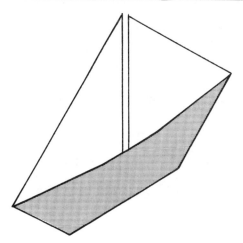

6 Turn it around to discover a sailboat!

Fish

This uncomplicated model is ideal for young children.

Concepts and vocabulary (*See also* page 4)

across

sideways

strip

slit

tail

nose

fish

halfway

Materials

Paper scraps cut into thin strips approximately 1 inch by 8 inches

Scissors

Additional suggestions

If you stop after Step 4, you have a flying fish. Hold it high in the air and let go. It will twirl its way to the floor.

Use the fish on a mobile or as a Christmas tree ornament.

Attach paper clips to the fish. Make a fishing pole by rolling a sheet of newspaper on the diagonal and tying a string and magnet to it. Go fishing!

How to fold the Fish

1. Make a cut on the upper right side. Cut halfway across, as shown.
   Repeat on the lower left side.

2. Bring the bottom slit up to meet the top slit. Push them into each other.

3. It looks like this.

4. Turn the fish sideways and pinch its nose flat.

5. Make little cuts on the tail pieces, as shown. Fill in the center with folded or rolled strips of paper.

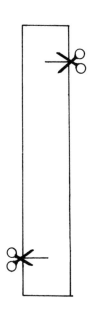

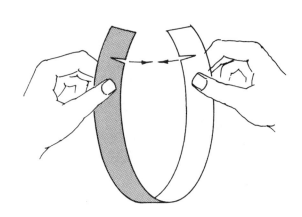

1 Make a cut on the upper right side. Cut halfway across, as shown.

Repeat on the lower left side.

2 Bring the bottom slit up to meet the top slit. Push them into each other.

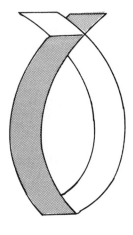

3 It looks like this.

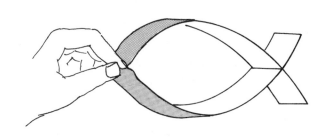

4 Turn the fish sideways and pinch its nose flat.

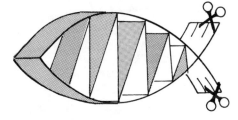

5 Make little cuts on the tail pieces, as shown. Fill in the center with folded or rolled strips of paper.

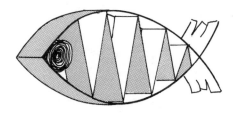

Alligator

Hint

You may wish to make a cardboard pattern of the alligator shape for the students to use.

Concepts and vocabulary (*See also* page 4)

half

through

slit

alligator

both

again

Materials

A 5-inch by 12-inch rectangle of construction paper

Pencil

Scissors

An additional suggestion

Find out about alligators and crocodiles. Compare them.

How to fold the Alligator

1. Put a rectangle of paper on the table with the long sides at the top and bottom.
   Fold the top edge down to meet the bottom edge.

2. Draw the alligator shape, as shown, using the folded edge for its back. Cut it out through both layers.

3. Draw short lines on its back. Cut the lines into slits on the folded edge.

4. Unfold and lay flat on the table.

5. Fold the slits backward.

6. Fold in half again, as shown.

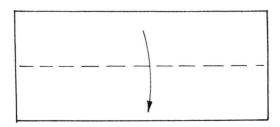

1 Put a rectangle of paper on the table with the long sides at the top and bottom.

Fold the top edge down to meet the bottom edge.

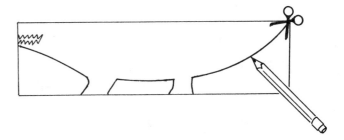

2 Draw the alligator shape, as shown, using the folded edge for its back. Cut it out through both layers.

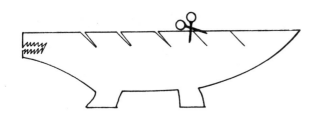

3 Draw short lines on its back. Cut the lines into slits on the folded edge.

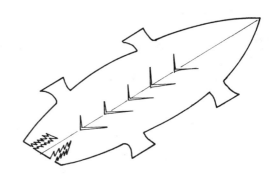

4 Unfold and lay flat on the table.

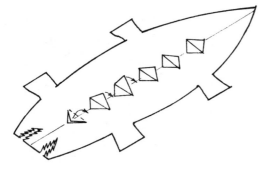

5 Fold the slits backward.

6 Fold in half again, as shown.

Canoe

The completed canoe has two pockets inside. Silhouettes of sailors can be placed in each pocket.

Concepts and vocabulary (*See also* page 4)

canoe

Materials

An 8½-inch by 11-inch sheet of paper

An additional suggestion

Use the canoe on a bulletin board showing Indian life.

How to fold the Canoe

1. Put a rectangle of paper on the table with the long edges at the top and bottom. Fold the bottom of the rectangle up to meet the top. Press flat. Unfold.

2. Fold the top of the rectangle down to meet the center crease. Fold the bottom of the rectangle up to meet the center crease.

3. Turn over. It looks like this.

4. Fold in all four corners to the center crease, as shown.

5. Fold the top down to meet the bottom.

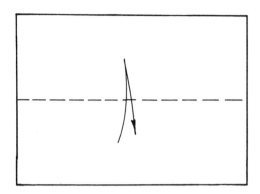

1 Put a rectangle of paper on the table with the long edges at the top and bottom. Fold the bottom of the rectangle up to meet the top. Press flat. Unfold.

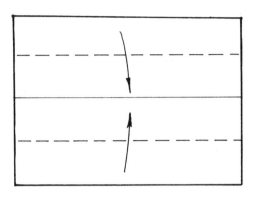

2 Fold the top of the rectangle down to meet the center crease. Fold the bottom of the rectangle up to meet the center crease.

3 Turn over. It looks like this.

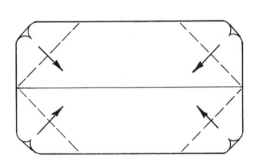

4 Fold in all four corners to the center crease, as shown.

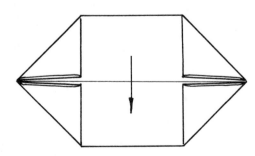

5 Fold the top down to meet the bottom.

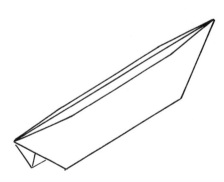

Whale

Hint

In Step 3, be sure to fold the entire lower edge over to meet the center crease, not just the corners.

Concepts and vocabulary (*See also* page 4)

sideways

end

tail

ice-cream cone

find

Materials

A 6-inch or larger square of thin paper

Additional suggestions

Make the whale as a Father's Day card "for a whale of a Dad."

Discuss other fish-like mammals (dolphin, porpoise).

How to fold the Whale

1. Put a square of paper on the table so it looks like a diamond.

2. Fold the left point over to meet the right point. Unfold, and find the center crease.

3. Fold the lower left and right sides to meet the center crease.

4. It looks like an ice-cream cone. Now fold the top point down, as shown.

5. Fold the right side over to meet the left side.

6. Put your finger on the bottom point as you turn the whale sideways.

7. Fold the end point up to make a tail.

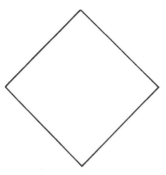

1 Put a square of paper on the table so it looks like a diamond.

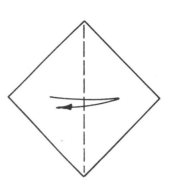

2 Fold the left point over to meet the right point. Unfold, and find the center crease.

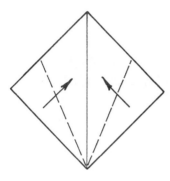

3 Fold the lower left and right sides to meet the center crease.

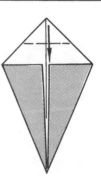

4 It looks like an ice-cream cone. Now fold the top point down, as shown.

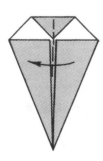

5 Fold the right side over to meet the left side.

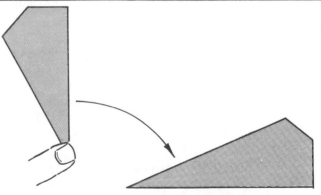

6 Put your finger on the bottom point as you turn the whale sideways.

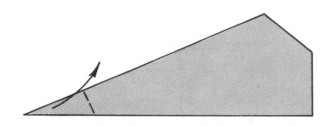

7 Fold the end point up to make a tail.

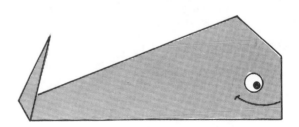

Swan

Hint

It may help the students to make a better cone shape if you call the center crease a "stop line" at Step 2.

Concepts and vocabulary (*See also* page 4)

swan

folded

half

Materials

A 6-inch or larger square of thin paper

Additional suggestions

Use the swan for a Christmas tree ornament, mobile, and gift-box decoration.

Make a small swan for a place card, a medium-sized one for a party favor, and a large one for a centerpiece. Teach the concepts of small, medium, and large.

How to fold the Swan

1. Put a square of paper on the table so it looks like a diamond. Fold the left point over to meet the right point. Crease. Unfold.

2. Fold the lower left side in to meet the center crease. Repeat with the lower right side.

3. It looks like an ice-cream cone. Turn it over.
   Now it looks like a kite.

4. Fold the left and right folded sides in to meet the center crease.

5. Fold the narrow point over to meet the wide point.

6. Fold the narrow point down to the dot, as shown, to make the swan's head.
   Fold in half by bringing the sides backward. (The left side meets the right side.)

7. Hold the swan as shown. Pinch its neck and lift it away from the body.

8. Pull up the head. Pinch flat at the dots, as shown.

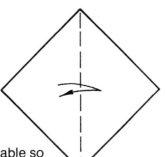

1 Put a square of paper on the table so it looks like a diamond. Fold the left point over to meet the right point. Crease. Unfold.

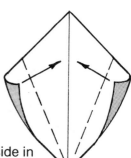

2 Fold the lower left side in to meet the center crease. Repeat with the lower right side.

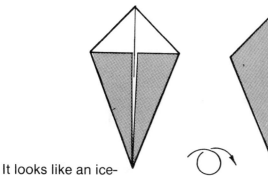

3 It looks like an ice-cream cone. Turn it over. Now it looks like a kite.

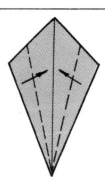

4 Fold the left and right folded sides in to meet the center crease.

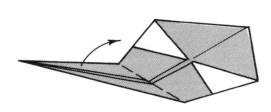

5 Fold the narrow point over to meet the wide point.

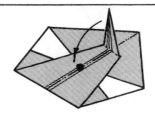

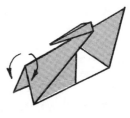

6 Fold the narrow point down to the dot, as shown, to make the swan's head.

Fold in half by bringing the sides backward. (The left side meets the right side.)

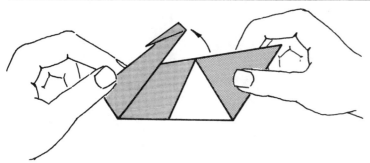

7 Hold the swan as shown. Pinch its neck and lift it away from the body.

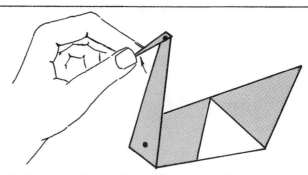

8 Pull up the head. Pinch flat at the dots, as shown.

Viking Hat

Hints

In Step 4, make sure the points are folded so they point straight up, rather than out to the side.

If you turn the model over after Step 5, it looks like the head of a fox.

Concepts and vocabulary (*See also* page 4)

other

Viking

Materials

A 15-inch square of thin paper. (Foil-backed gift wrap is ideal.)

An additional suggestion

Discuss sailors "now and then."

How to fold the Viking Hat

1. Put a square of paper on the table so it looks like a diamond. Fold the top point down to meet the bottom point, forming a triangle.

2. Fold the left point down to the bottom point.

3. Repeat with the right point.

4. Fold the bottom left point up to the left dot, as shown.

5. Repeat with the bottom right point.

6. There are two layers at the bottom. Lift up only the top layer as far as it will go. Crease.

7. Turn over. Repeat on the other side.

1 Put a square of paper on the table so it looks like a diamond. Fold the top point down to meet the bottom point, forming a triangle.

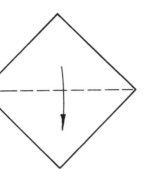

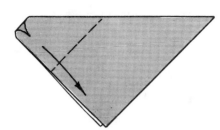

2 Fold the left point down to the bottom point.

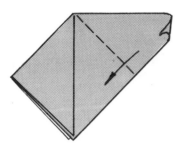

3 Repeat with the right point.

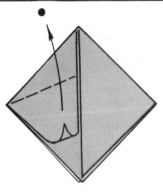

4 Fold the bottom left point up to the left dot, as shown.

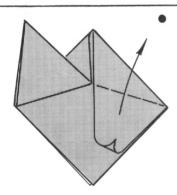

5 Repeat with the bottom right point.

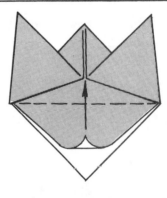

6 There are two layers at the bottom. Lift up only the top layer as far as it will go. Crease.

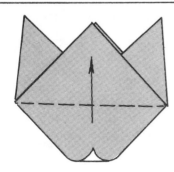

7 Turn over. Repeat on the other side.

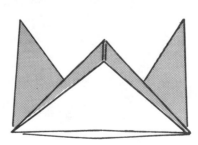

Goldfish

Hint

Fold the Viking Hat before you make this model. The folds are the same up to Step 6.

Concepts and vocabulary (*See also* page 4)

together

goldfish

thumbs

flatten

index finger

Materials

A square of thin paper, colored on one side (wrapping paper is ideal)

An additional suggestion

Make several goldfish. Use them to make a mobile.

How to fold the Goldfish

1. Begin with the white side up. Put the paper on the table so it looks like a diamond. Fold the top point down to meet the bottom point, forming a triangle.

2. Fold the left point down to the bottom point.

3. Repeat with the other point.

4. Fold the left point up to the left dot, as shown. Repeat with the right point.

5. There are two layers at the bottom. Lift up only the top layer as far as it will go. Crease.

6. Put your index finger inside, all the way up to the top, to help open the model.

7. Now put your thumbs inside and press the sides together. Flatten the model.

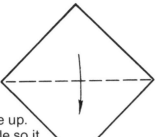

1 Begin with the white side up. Put the paper on the table so it looks like a diamond.
Fold the top point down to meet the bottom point, forming a triangle.

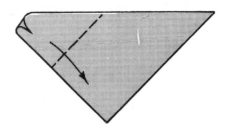

2 Fold the left point down to the bottom point.

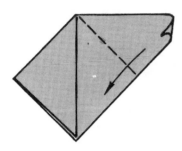

3 Repeat with the other point.

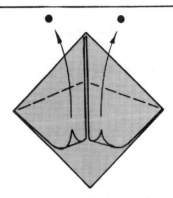

4 Fold the left point up to the left dot, as shown. Repeat with the right point.

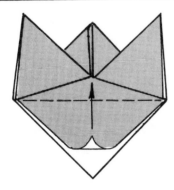

5 There are two layers at the bottom. Lift up only the top layer as far as it will go. Crease.

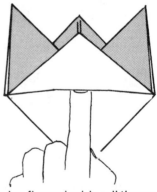

6 Put your index finger inside, all the way up to the top, to help open the model.

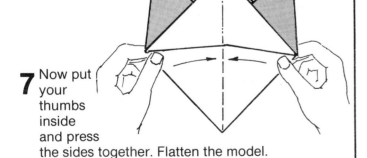

7 Now put your thumbs inside and press the sides together. Flatten the model.

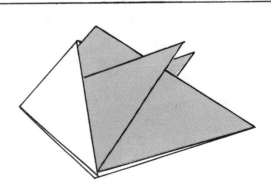

Crab

This model is a bit tricky for very young children to complete. Have them fold the Pecking Bird before attempting the Crab.

Concepts and vocabulary (*See also* page 4)

further

shell

reach inside

peck

crab

Materials

Two 6-inch or larger squares of thin paper

An additional suggestion

Discuss other animals that have shells.

How to fold the Crab

1. Put one square of paper on the table so it looks like a diamond.
Fold the left point over to meet the right point. Crease. Unfold.

2. Fold the lower left and right sides up to meet the center crease.

3. Fold the upper left and right sides down to meet the center crease.

4. Fold the top point down to the dot, as shown.

5. Fold the bottom point up to the dot, as shown.

6. Fold in half by bringing the left side over to meet the right side.

(continued on page 156)

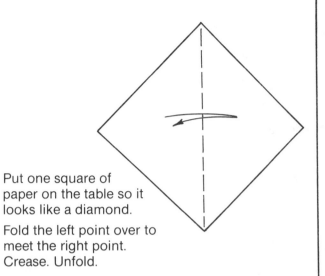

1 Put one square of paper on the table so it looks like a diamond.

Fold the left point over to meet the right point. Crease. Unfold.

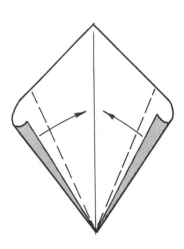

2 Fold the lower left and right sides up to meet the center crease.

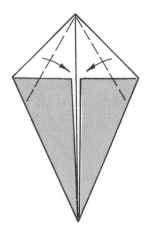

3 Fold the upper left and right sides down to meet the center crease.

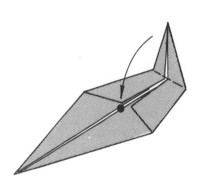

4 Fold the top point down to the dot, as shown.

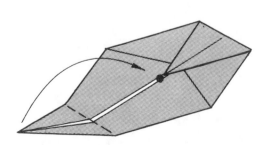

5 Fold the bottom point up to the dot, as shown.

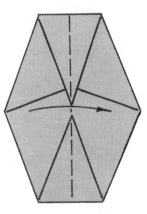

6 Fold in half by bringing the left side over to meet the right side.

How to fold the Crab (continued)

7. Pick it up, as shown.

8. Reach inside and pinch the long (leg) triangle together. Pull it up a little bit so it peeks out of the shell.

9. Pinch flat at the dot.

   Repeat with the long (leg) triangle at the other end.

10. Now repeat Steps 1 through 7 with the other square of paper. This time, at Steps 8 and 9, pull the legs out a little further, as shown.

11. Tuck the first piece inside the second piece, and stand the crab up on its legs.

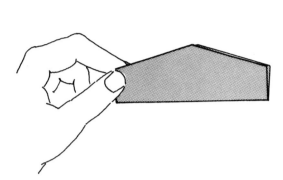

7 Pick it up, as shown.

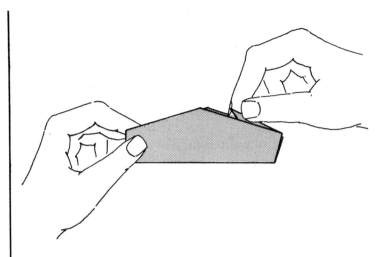

8 Reach inside and pinch the long (leg) triangle together. Pull it up a little bit so it peeks out of the shell.

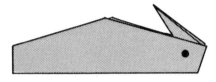

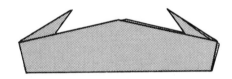

9 Pinch flat at the dot.
Repeat with the long (leg) triangle at the other end.

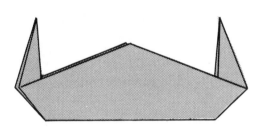

10 Now repeat Steps 1 through 7 with the other square of paper. This time, at Steps 8 and 9, pull the legs out a little further, as shown.

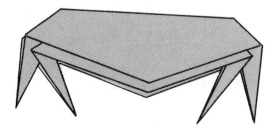

11 Tuck the first piece inside the second piece, and stand the crab up on its legs.

Frog

This complex model is not suitable for very young children.

Hint

Fold the frog yourself, so you can anticipate any problems the children might have.

Concepts and vocabulary (*See also* page 4)

together

jump

frog

Materials

A rectangle of stiff paper (for example, an index card)

An additional suggestion

Make a *Fun Folds* Wagon Base (p. 108). Have the frog "jump" into the box by pressing on its back.

How to fold the Frog

1. Put a rectangle of stiff paper on the table with the short edges at the top and bottom. Fold down the left top corner, as shown.

2. Unfold.

3. Fold down the right top corner, as shown.

4. Unfold.

5. Turn over.

6. Fold the top edge down to the bottom of the "letter X."

7. Unfold.

8. Fold the left side over to meet the right side. Unfold. Turn over.

9. It looks like this. Note the "mountain" and "valley" folds (see Symbols, p. 5).

(continued on page 160)

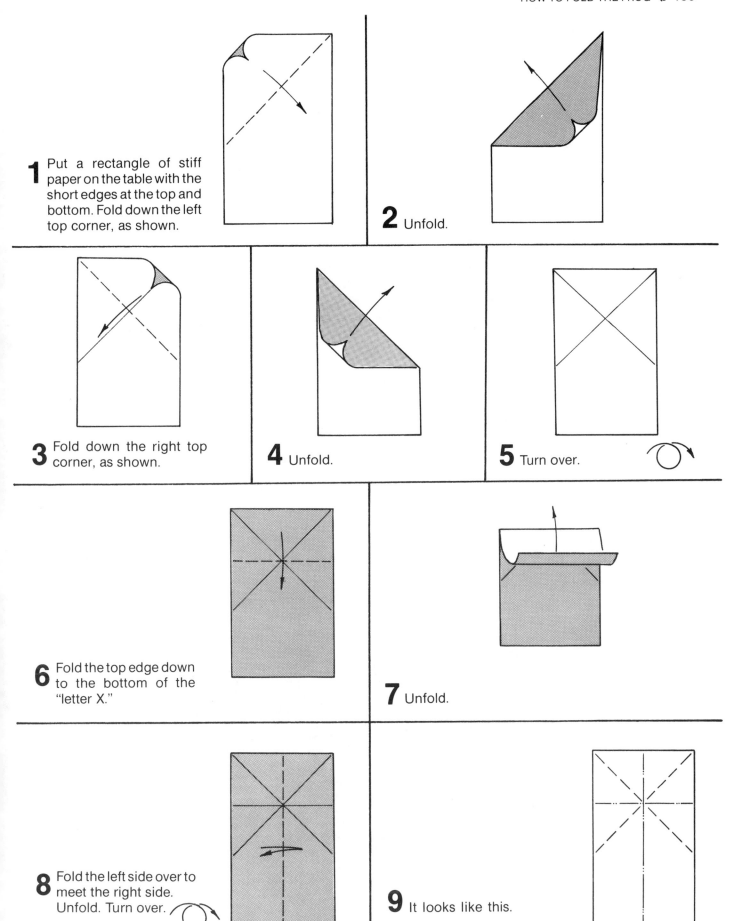

1 Put a rectangle of stiff paper on the table with the short edges at the top and bottom. Fold down the left top corner, as shown.

2 Unfold.

3 Fold down the right top corner, as shown.

4 Unfold.

5 Turn over.

6 Fold the top edge down to the bottom of the "letter X."

7 Unfold.

8 Fold the left side over to meet the right side. Unfold. Turn over.

9 It looks like this.

How to fold the Frog (continued)

10. Push the two dots together, as shown.

11. Press the top triangle flat. Now it looks like a house.

12. On the top layer, fold the left and right side points to the top.

13. Fold the left side in to meet the center crease. Repeat with the right side.

14. Fold the bottom up to meet the top.

15. Fold the top layer only, down to meet the bottom.

16. It looks like this. Turn over.

17. Press down on the frog's back, then let go. See it jump!

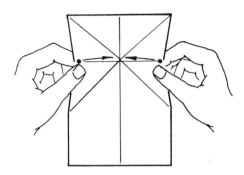

10 Push the two dots together, as shown.

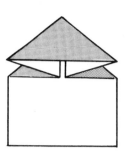

11 Press the top triangle flat. Now it looks like a house.

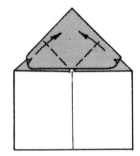

12 On the top layer, fold the left and right side points to the top.

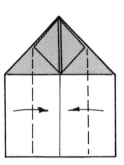

13 Fold the left side in to meet the center crease. Repeat with the right side.

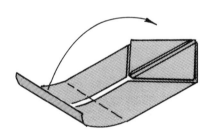

14 Fold the bottom up to meet the top.

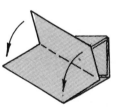

15 Fold the top layer only, down to meet the bottom.

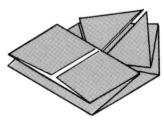

16 It looks like this. Turn over.

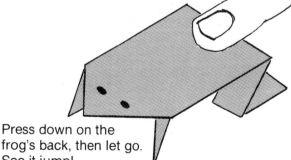

17 Press down on the frog's back, then let go. See it jump!

Additional Readings

Bank-Jensen, Thea. 1962. *Play with paper.* New York: The Macmillan Company.

Benjamin, Ranana. 1981. *Teaching with origami.* Great Neck, NY: R. B. Ventures.

Gray, Alice, and Kunihiko Kasahara. 1977. *The magic of paper folding.* Tokyo: Japan Publications, Inc.

Harbin, Robert. 1957. *Paper magic.* London: Charles T. Branford Company.

Honda, Isao. 1965. *The world of origami.* Tokyo: Japan Publications Trading Company.

Kaplan, Dorothy. 1971. *Perceptual development through paper folding.* Deal, NJ: Kimbo Educational Records.

Kasahara, Kunihiko. 1973. *Origami made easy.* Tokyo: Japan Publications, Inc.

Lewis, Shari, and Lillian Oppenheimer. 1962. *Folding paper puppets.* New York: Stein and Day.

_____. 1963. *Folding paper toys.* New York: Stein and Day.

_____. 1965. *Folding paper masks.* New York: E. P. Dutton & Co., Inc.

Soong, Maying. 1948. *The art of Chinese paper folding.* New York: Harcourt Brace & World.

Sugimura, Takaji. 1983. *Living origami.* Osaka, Japan: Hoikusha Publishing Co., Ltd.

Takahama, Toshie. 1972. *Origami flowers.* Tokyo: Yukishobo Co., Ltd.

_____. 1973. *Origami animals.* Tokyo: Yukishobo Co., Ltd.

_____. 1974. *Origami for displays.* Tokyo: Shufunotomo Co., Ltd.

Temko, Florence. 1974. *Paper: Folded, cut, sculpted.* London: Collier Macmillan Publishers.

Temko, Florence, and Elaine Simon. 1968. *Paper folding to begin with.* New York: Bobbs-Merrill Company, Inc.

SPEECH, LANGUAGE, AND READING WORKSHEETS: Fun with Language   (1983)
by Margaret F. Smith

Complete your total speech program with these 81 copiable pages. Here are effective and economical worksheet activities to help you integrate your therapy program with your students' classroom work—valuable for home carryover, too. Each page presents a task clearly with simple line drawings. The 3-ring binder offers easy organization.

Catalog No. 4636-Y   **$24.95**

GET THE PICTURE? Basic Exercises in Verbal Communication   (1984)
by Debbie Harrison Wieser

This portable kit features five delightful posters with colorful illustrations on these topics—Weather, Pets, Opposites, People, and Doing Things. Pick any of the 148 Cue Cards and you'll have ready-to-use lessons for your therapy sessions. The 32 Activity Cards pinpoint specific language skills.

Catalog No. 7045-Y   **$25**

TALK IT UP: 40 Games for Language Reinforcement and Remediation   (1984)
by Dianne Schoenfeld Barad

Here's a handy folder of high-interest activities to boost language skills. You can expand your students' verbal expression and save your planning time with these photocopiable game-sheets. These ready-to-use activities focus on classification, association, and using descriptive language.

Catalog No. 7021-Y   **$18.95**

FAMILIAR ACTIONS AND OBJECTS: A Go-Fish Card Game
for Early Language Development   (1984)   *by Ann Marquis and Nancy Lewis*

You can focus on pragmatic language skills with your younger students. These 90 pairs of appealing cards present everyday sights and happenings. Your students must use nouns, verbs, and adjectives to tell about each card. The game's turn-taking format encourages effective descriptions and attentive listening.

Catalog No. 7060-Y   **$35**

HOT AIR BALLOONS: A Go-Fish Card Game for Intermediate Language Development   (1984)
by Ann Marquis

Use these 90 pairs of full-color photo cards to develop language interaction skills in your students. This supplementary material emphasizes turn-taking, topic maintenance, use of specific vocabulary, and other pragmatic language abilities. These 180 colorful cards offer the "instant interest" of hot air balloons. Students are motivated to describe the cards accurately. Each of the five decks presents cards for a particular level of difficulty.

Catalog No. 7059-Y   **$35**

Communication Skill Builders, Inc. ®
3830 E. Bellevue/P.O. Box 42050
Tucson, Arizona 85733
(602) 323-7500